Tra

Amin Yagmuri

Translation and Interference

A Case Study of Azerbaijani Literary System in Iran

LAP LAMBERT Academic Publishing

Impressum / Imprint
Bibliografische Information der Deutschen Nationalbibliothek: Die Deutsche Nationalbibliothek verzeichnet diese Publikation in der Deutschen Nationalbibliografie; detaillierte bibliografische Daten sind im Internet über http://dnb.d-nb.de abrufbar.
Alle in diesem Buch genannten Marken und Produktnamen unterliegen warenzeichen-, marken- oder patentrechtlichem Schutz bzw. sind Warenzeichen oder eingetragene Warenzeichen der jeweiligen Inhaber. Die Wiedergabe von Marken, Produktnamen, Gebrauchsnamen, Handelsnamen, Warenbezeichnungen u.s.w. in diesem Werk berechtigt auch ohne besondere Kennzeichnung nicht zu der Annahme, dass solche Namen im Sinne der Warenzeichen- und Markenschutzgesetzgebung als frei zu betrachten wären und daher von jedermann benutzt werden dürften.

Bibliographic information published by the Deutsche Nationalbibliothek: The Deutsche Nationalbibliothek lists this publication in the Deutsche Nationalbibliografie; detailed bibliographic data are available in the Internet at http://dnb.d-nb.de.
Any brand names and product names mentioned in this book are subject to trademark, brand or patent protection and are trademarks or registered trademarks of their respective holders. The use of brand names, product names, common names, trade names, product descriptions etc. even without a particular marking in this works is in no way to be construed to mean that such names may be regarded as unrestricted in respect of trademark and brand protection legislation and could thus be used by anyone.

Coverbild / Cover image: www.ingimage.com

Verlag / Publisher:
LAP LAMBERT Academic Publishing
ist ein Imprint der / is a trademark of
OmniScriptum GmbH & Co. KG
Heinrich-Böcking-Str. 6-8, 66121 Saarbrücken, Deutschland / Germany
Email: info@lap-publishing.com

Herstellung: siehe letzte Seite /
Printed at: see last page
ISBN: 978-3-659-47976-2

Zugl. / Approved by: Department of Foreign Languages, East Azarbaijan Science and Research Branch, Islamic Azad University,Tabriz,Iran, Diss., 2013

Table of Contents

1

List of Tables

List of Figures

To the people of my Homeland

With *Love*

Acknowledgements

Firstly, I would like to thank dear Dr. Sayyed Muhammad Karimi Behbahani, my supervisor, for his insightful and perceptive guidance. Secondly, my thanks go for Dr. Bahloul Salmani for his useful suggestions. I also would like to thank my dear friends, Ehsan Alipour and Arezou Farajiani, for their useful comments, edits and kind supports. I am grateful for having supportive friends.

Finally and most importantly, I would like to appreciate the care and kindness of my parents, Darioush and Azizeh, whom have always supported and encouraged me during this project.

Chapter One:
Introduction

1.1. Introduction

"There is not one single literature which did not emerge through interference with a more established literature; and no literature could manage without interference at one time or another during its history."

(Even-Zohar, 1990, p.55)

Even-Zohar (1990 & 2012) believed that interference is present and unavoidable in the literary history of almost every literature. He claimed that most human societies and literatures have come into being through interference with other societies. It is the interference, according to him, that helps the literatures to survive and change. However, there must be some sort of contact between two literatures in order to result into interference. "Naturally, a precondition for interference must be some kind of contact-whether direct or indirect- but the opposite is not necessarily true; contact may occur without generating any substantial interference" (Even-Zohar, 2010, p. 53).

According to this presupposition, the relation between the literary system of Azerbaijani and Persian could be studied according to the laws of interference. Iran is a multicultural country that is home for different cultural and lingual groups. Azerbaijanis are one of these groups that live mostly in the north-western part of Iran. These people study Persian language and lack proficiency in their own language. However, there are some individuals who can produce literary texts in this literature. The writing system of the given language is different from that of Persian, i.e., Turkic with Arabic alphabet.

As a consequence of the treaty of Turkmenchay in 1822, Azerbaijan has been divided into two regions of South and North Azerbaijan and the river Aras was set as the border of these two regions (Burançç& Alkaya, 2009). Since then, according to Yavuz

8

Akpınar (1994) the literature of the Republic of Azerbaijan has been considered as "North Azerbaijani literature" while the literature of Azerbaijanis in Iran has been called "South Azerbaijani literature" (p.17).Since then, the official language of Iran has been Persian and the literary system of Azerbaijani in Iran has been considered as the literature of a minority language. Indeed, there seems to be literary contacts between these two literatures; therefore, the possible interferences between the literary system of Azerbaijani and Persian in Iran have been studied in the present book.

1.2. Statement of the Problem

The authors are providing the research with the data following the framework of literary polysystem model. Evan-Zohar (1990) hypothesized that "when a researcher is confronted with an unclear situation, that is when one must choose for a certain case between the hypothesis of separate development vs. the hypothesis of interference, unless refutable on very clear grounds, in spite of our accepted inclinations, priority ought to be given to the interference hypothesis"(1990, pp. 50-51). In other words, if one wants to study a literary-unknown system of a region, one should presuppose that literature as developed through interference. According to this, the study presupposes that literary system of Azerbaijani in Iran is a interfered with by other literatures; thus, it can be studied according to the laws of literary interference. The scope of the paper covers the number of the translations imported into the literature of Azerbaijani of Iran after the Islamic Revolution in 1979. The present study wishes to examine the validity of the four hypotheses of the literary interference in the case of Azerbaijani literary system. In order to achieve this, the writers are going to examine the number of the imported texts into the literature of Azerbaijani of Iran and scrutinize the four hypotheses of literary interference; (a) Interference is mostly unilateral, (b) Contacts will sooner or later generate interference if no resisting conditions arise, (c) Interference occurs when a system is in need of items unavailable within its own repertoire, (d) Contacts may take place with only one part of the target literature; it may then proceed to other parts.

Itamar Even-Zohar (2010) has stated that, "in the case of minority groups physically living among majority groups, being exposed daily to the culture of the majority, interference may be much more powerful than in those cases where the target can to some degree avoid the source" (p.53). Moreover, he has added that "interference functions for all sizes and levels of social configurations: families, clans, tribes, 'classes,' ethnic groups, geographically organized groups as well as nations, or groups of nations" (2010, p.54).

The authors are providing the research with the data following the framework of literary polysystem model. Therefore, the literature of Azerbaijani in Iran can be studied as a social configuration according to the laws of literary interference. Even-Zohar has introduced two types of interference, namely direct and indirect interference. In the first type, the interference occurs without intermediaries and the target agents can access to the source language literature. To access to the source is an easy task because they know it well. This is like the case of Azerbaijani-Persian in Iran. As a matter of fact, Azerbaijanis living in Iran study Persian language, the official language, at schools and become proficient in this language.

In the second type of the interference, i.e., indirect, some channels take the role of intermediary to achieve the source literature (2010).This also can be seen in the case of Azerbaijani literature of Iran. How the indirect literary interference, mostly translation, functions in the case of the literary system of Azerbaijani in Iran is a special case that can be studied.

The case of this literary system in Iran is provocative enough to be studied according to the laws of literary interference. The existing interference, as Even-Zohar (2010) has claimed it as always imminent, in the case of this literature, needs to be studied in order to be defined according to the polysystem theory and literary interference.

1.3. Significance of the Study

The unique case of the literary system of Azerbaijani in Iran is important to be studied, because it seems to overlap with the study of the minority languages. It also is a unique case to be studied within the laws of literary interference of polysystem theory. Those researchers that are interested in the minority language studies and polysystem theory will find this research helpful. It is hoped that the present study can give a better understanding of the impact of translation on Azerbaijani literature in Iran. Therefore, it will be useful for those who are involved in the literature of this language, those who translate into or from this language and those who study its literary system. It is also hoped that the findings of the current study would improve the academic level of translational methods for scholars working on Azerbaijani literature and translation. In addition, the findings of the study are expected to provide insights into central issues to polysystem studies.

1.4. Purpose of the Study

Itamar Even-Zohar (2010) has introduced three sets of hypotheses. The first set of the hypotheses deals with the nature (what), the second set with the reason (why), and the third set with the process (how) of the literary interference. The authors have selected four hypotheses out of these to study the case of the literary system of Azerbaijani of Iran. These hypotheses are; (a) Interference is mostly unilateral, (b) Contacts will sooner or later generate interference if no resisting conditions arise, (c) Interference occurs when a system is in need of items unavailable within its own repertoire, (d) Contacts may take place with only one part of the target literature; it may then proceed to other parts. The authors are providing the research with the data

11

following the framework of literary polysystem model and also the data provided in this study. The aim of this study is to apply these four hypotheses to the literature of this language and find out which of these hypotheses holds true in its literature. Consequently, the aim of the research is to define the role of translation in the literary system of Azerbaijani in Iran according to the data provided in this study. This study is not intended to generalize statements about the condition of translation in this system. To describe how translation functions in this literary system according to the provided data in this study is the main goal of the research.

1.5. Research Questions

In the case of the literary system of Azerbaijani in Iran:

a) Is interference mostly unilateral?

b) Does contact eventually generate interference in the absence of resisting condition?

c) Does interference occur for the unavailable items within the literary system?

d) Does contact occur with only one part of the target literature?

1.6. Theoretical Framework

Itamar Even-Zohar (2010, p.52) introduced interference as "a relation (ship) between literatures, whereby a certain literature A (a source literature) may become a source of direct or indirect transfer for another literature B (a target literature)". He (1990, p.55) has distinguished between two major states of literary systems. The first state, according to him, is relatively *independent*, whereas the second is *dependent*. In the first instance, a literature develops within its own spheres. In the second case, that of "dependent" systems, an external system may be a major condition for the very existence and development of such a literary system. He believes that this normally occurs either when a literature is young, that is the process of emergence, or when

12

conditions within it have created a certain situation which cannot be dealt with by the relevant literature exclusively--or mainly--by means of its own sources.

Even-Zohar (2010) has introduced three sets of hypotheses in the literary interference. The first set of the hypotheses deals with the general principles (what), the second set with the conditions (why), and the third set with the processes and procedures (how) of the literary interference.

These sets of laws according to him are governing laws with various degrees of validity of interference. Generally, he put forth three groups of aspects:

General principles of interference

1. Interference is always imminent.

2. Interference is mostly unilateral.

3. Interference may be restricted to certain domains.

Conditions for the emergence and occurrence of interference

4. Contacts will sooner or later generate interference if no resisting conditions arise.

5. Interference occurs when a system is in need of items unavailable within its own repertoire.

6. A source literature is selected by dominance.

7. A source literature is selected by prestige.

Processes and procedures of interference

8. Contacts may take place with only one part of the target literature; it may then proceed to other parts.

9. An appropriated repertoire does not necessarily maintain source literature functions.

The authors are providing the research with the data following the framework of literary polysystem model. According to the unique case of the literary system of

13

Azerbaijani in Iran four of these hypotheses have been selected to be applied to this study. These hypotheses are:

a) Interference is mostly unilateral (1.2)

b) Contacts will sooner or later generate interference if no resisting conditions arise (2.1)

c) Interference occurs when a system is in need of items unavailable within its own repertoire (2.2).

d) Contacts may take place with only one part of the target literature; it may then proceed to other parts (3.1)

These four hypotheses have been selected because authors considered them more homogeneous in the case of literary system of Azerbaijani of Iran. The aim of this study is to apply these four hypotheses to literature of this language and find out which of these hypotheses holds true in this literature.

1.7. Limitations and Delimitations

This research has some limitations and delimitations: collecting a complete list of Azerbaijani translated texts seem to be unpractical. The main source of collecting data is the national library and archives of the Islamic Republic of Iran. Indeed, all the books and translations are not recorded in this site. Therefore, the authors are aware of this fact and know that the provided data should not be considered as complete and permanent.

The extent to which the researcher will study the translated texts is limited to the printed and digitally-in-Arabic texts in Azerbaijani literary system of Iran. Therefore, the number of translated and original books will be studied since the Islamic Revolution of Iran. The authors will collect only the source language, target language, genre, and year of the publication of the books. The data will be only the published books and the research will exclude the magazines, CDs, newsletter and journals.

1.8. Definitions of the Key Terms

Interference: "contacts can be defined as "a relation (ship) between cultures, whereby a certain culture A (a source culture) may become a source of direct or indirect transfer for another culture B (a target literature)." Once this possibility is realized, interference can be said to have occurred. Interference is thus a procedure emerging in the environment of contacts, one where transfer has taken place" (p.52).

Literary System of Azerbaijani in Iran: In this research the literary system of Azerbaijani in Iran refers to the literature of Turks that live in Iran and use Arabic alphabet as their writing system. Random House Dictionary (1990) defines Azerbaijani as "a member of an Azerbaijani-speaking people of Azerbaijan and of the Iranian provinces of Azerbaijan" and also "the Turkic language of the Azerbaijani, written with Cyrillic [now Latin] letters in Azerbaijan and with Arabic letters in Iran". Azerbaijani is a major language in the Republic of Azerbaijan, while it is considered a minority language in Iran. In addition, Yavuz Akpınar (1994) has introduced the literature of the Republic of Azerbaijan as "North Azerbaijani lirerarture" while the literature of Azerbaijanis in Iran as "South Azerbaijani literature" (p.17). However, in the present research Azerbaijnai of Iran is going to be used.

Resisting Condition: Itamar Even-Zohar (2010) belived that "sometimes, highly nationalistic societies reject any interference, because it is felt to be a threat to national integrity." He has added that various French intellectuals like "Zola, Daudet, and Goncourts (to name just a few) violently objected to the introduction of any high-culture products from abroad, trying to demonstrate the incompatibility of foreign culture with 'the French spirit'" (p.60). Throughout this research, by resisting condition authors refer to any condition in which society, intellectuals or circles attempt to resist the occurrence of literary interference.

Repertoire: By repertoire, Even-Zohar (2010) meant "the aggregate of rules and materials which govern both the making and holding, or production and consumption, of any given product" (p.17). In this research, the above definition is used.

Chapter Two:
Review of Literature

2.1. Overview

This chapter is included of three main parts. The first part deals with general principles of the polysystem theory developed by Itamar Even-Zohar. Then, the laws of the interference (2010) has been presented and defined one by one. The second part deals with four works on similar conditions of the literary system of Azerbaijani in Iran that are developed and studied according to polysystem theory. In the second part Mahmoud Kayyal (2008), Wang Dongfeng (2008), Noriko Matsunaga-Watson (2005), and Ehsan Alipour's (2012) works have been paraphrased shortly. In the third part, literary, geographical, historical and lingual status of Azerbaijani in Iran has been presented.

2.2. General Principles of the Polysystem

Itamar Even-Zohar in his publication on the well-known Polysystem theory defined the purpose of the polysystem as a means of explication of "a system as dynamic and heterogeneous in opposition to the synchronistic approach." According to him, Polysystem theory also consists of "the greater complexity of structuredness;" the function of a system does not necessitate the uniformity (1990a, p.12). Developed since 1969 through 2010, the polysystem theory has its roots in Russian Formalism. Unlike Russian Formalism which "was mostly designed to deal with problems of literature," Polysystem theory "eventually strives to account for larger complexes than literature" (Even-Zohar, 1990a, pp. 1-2). To work with Polysystem theory one needs to accept it as a whole theory, which is considered by Even-Zohar as "a network of independent hypotheses" (p. 4). Consequently, if one uses Polysystem theory as a tool to classify the texts and writers, and one does not take into account the correlation between repertoire and system, or between products and consumption, then one changes it to a partial, and unhelpful theory(1990a). Therefore, to study a system in correlation with other systems, one needs to consider the existence of the rules governing the relation between products and consumption. In other words, the texts and writers cannot be considered as the only subjects of the research in studying a system in the framework of Polysystem theory. Even-Zohar has proposed that "if one accepts the polysystem hypotheses, then one must also accept that the historical study of literary polysystems cannot confine itself to the so-called 'masterpieces,' even if some would consider them the only raison d'être of literary studies in the first place" (1990a, p.13).

According to him, in Polysystem theory systems move from one stratum to the other, i.e., it is the conflict of achieving the central stratum. Systems, in this centrifugal vs. centripetal motion, tend to move from periphery to the central strata, while pushing the others from central ones to the peripheral strata. In the conflict of achieving the central position, one must not consider the struggle over only one center and one periphery, but they need to recognize polysystem as hypothesizing several strata (1990a). He has also stated that this fact had not been detected before; thus, no one could know about the value of the variety of strata. When a change happened, i.e., the exchange of the phenomena between the strata; one could have an individual imagination of the occurrence. Therefore, the result was that the transfer stayed unsolvable and indefinable. Polysystem theory, with its hypotheses, is occupied with the questions which deal with the reason of the transfer of phenomena within the systems (1990a). In other words, polysystem has resulted into an approach to define the previously-unknown phenomena in heterogeneous systems.

According to Itamar Even-Zohar, strata are of two kinds; namely canonized and non-canonized. The first refers to the literary norms and works that are seen as legitimate by the circles within a culture, while the latter is considered as the illegitimate one. The concept of canonicity should not be considered as "good" vs. "bad" literature, and also, one should not think that it is a matter of inherent. He also believed that there is no non-stratified human society upon the earth. In all human systems , one can see the tensions between the canonized and non-canonized strata (1990a).Even Zohar claimed that "the canonized repertoire of any system would very likely stagnate after a certain time if not for competition from non-canonized challengers, which often threaten to replace them," (1990, p.16). Afterwards, he added that if no pressures are allowed release, the system often either departs and move to another one, or collapses by means of a revolution (Even-Zohar, 1990a). Therefore, from above, we can consider the existence and dynamism of a system through the tensions of the strata. Systems, within which there is no tension, tend to be petrified gradually.

Canon, introduced before as the legitimate, controls the whole polysystem. The group which cannot adhere to the properties canonized by it, or the repertoire of canonized properties, "both the group and its canonized repertoire are pushed aside by some other group, which makes its way to the center by canonizing a different repertoire". The groups which still adhere to the displayed canonized repertoire hardly ever can govern the center of the polysystem (Even-Zohar, 1990a, p.17).

In his 1990 publication, Itamar Even Zohar has defined *repertoire* as "the aggregate of laws and elements (single, bound, or total models) that govern the production of texts" (p.17). He has added that the system to which a repertoire belongs, the repertoire can be either canonized or non-canonized, may possess a central or peripheral position. It is the relations that a literary repertoire obtains in the (poly) system which determines the status of that repertoire. In addition, the conservatory or innovatory elites can support the canonized repertoire (1990a). It is likely that the repertoire which is supported by one of these two groups will produce the texts according to the tastes of its supporter. Similarly, Even-Zohar asserted that "texts and repertoire are only partial

20

manifestations of literature," and "rather than playing a role in the processes of canonization, are the outcome of these processes" (1990a, pp. 18-19). It becomes clear, from the above facts, that in studying a literary system, one should not assume the texts and repertoire as the only variable of his studying but he must take into consideration the principles and circles governing the given system. Text should be considered as only the outcomes of the literature.

Moreover, two different uses of the term "canonicity" have been distinguished by Even-Zohar, "one referring to the level of texts, the other to the level of models". For him, in the former case, " a certain text is accepted as a finalized product and inserted into a set of sanctified texts literature (culture) wants to preserve," which may be called "static canonicity", while in the latter case, "which may be called dynamic canonicity, a certain literary model manages to establish itself as a productive principle in the system through the latter's repertoire" (1990a, p.19).

The static canon as Even-Zohar held "is a primary condition for any system to be recognized as a distinct activity in culture" (1990a). From above, it is clear that the writers struggle to hold their texts in the static canon. What really matters for these writers is that they want their texts to be accepted and recognized as "a manifestation, a successful actualization" of the model that governs the dynamic canon. Also, Even-Zohar warned that "it would be a terrible disappointment for writers to have their particular texts accepted but their literary models rejected" (p.19). This situation can mean that these writers have lost their position as innovative authors. No writer at all, as Itamar Even-Zohar has concluded, can stand being his texts recognized as the great pieces while his model rejected as insufficient one to be followed. This can cause these writers to lose their contemporary position, which is a move from center to periphery, despite the fact that their texts are accepted (1990a).

Even-Zohar discussed that specific procedures are involved in the process of transfer. Similarly, he has proposed the opposition between "primary" and "secondary" types, i.e., opposition between "innovativeness" and "conservatism." He defined the secondary type as a "highly predictable" repertoire that is "established and all derivative models pertaining to it are constructed in full accordance with what it allows." On the other hand, the primary type, according to Even-Zohar, has been defined as a "less predictable" repertoire in which the precondition is "the discontinuity of established models." If the primary repertoire is perpetuated," when a primary model becomes dominant in the repertoire and subsequently in the (poly) system," the system bears a transfer from a primary model to a secondary one, that is from the innovatory to a conservative model. Even-Zohar concluded that "once there is a takeover, the new repertoire will not admit elements which are likely to endanger its dominance in the system. The process of 'secondariztion' of the primary thus turns out to be unavoidable" (1990a, pp. 20-22).

The above mentioned properties and principles not only hold true for the intra-relations but for inter-relations. "These inter-relations involve two kinds of adjacent systems: a larger whole belonging to the same community, and a whole, or its parts which belongs to other communities, either of the same order (sort) or not" (Even-Zohar, 1990a, p.22).

According to Even-Zohar, Polysystem theory can "deal with the particular conditions under which a certain literature may be interfered with by another literature, as result of which properties are transferred from one polysytem to another." Also, it is the polysystem theory which can study the processes of interference. Even-Zohar has contradicted the common belief about the interference and has highlighted that it "often takes place via peripheries" (1990a, p. 25).

2.3.   Laws of Literary Interference

According to Itamar Even-Zohar, "interference cannot be divorced from literary history, since it is part of the historical existence of any cultural system" (1990, p.54).

22

He defined interference as " a relation (ship) between literatures, whereby a certain literature A (a source literature) may become a source of direct or indirect transfer for another literature B (a target literature)" (p.52). He has emphasized that by literature he meant "the totality of the activities involved with the literary system that is meant." Even-Zohar argued that "it is not even repertoire which is the most decisive component participating in a specific interference relationship" (p. 54). According to him:

The role and function of literature, the rule of the game of the literary institution, the nature of literary criticism and scholarship, the relations between religious, political, and other activities within culture and literary production--all may be modeled in a given culture in relation to some other system. (1990, pp. 54-55)

He has inferred that reducing interference to just the seemingly more visible level of the text or even of the model(s) behind it would be inadequate. As Even-Zohar has distinguished, interference can be either "unilateral" or "bilateral", the former functioning for one literature and the latter for both. This depends on "the state of each of system involved." Similarly, he has recommended that distinguishing between two major states of literary systems, namely independent and dependent can be of some help. He referred to the first state as "a relatively established system" and to the second as "a non-established system" (p.55).

According to Even-Zohar's distinction, in the independent state, "a literature develops within its own spheres." He has claimed that an outside system or individual, sometimes, may be of some importance for it. For example, he has introduced the case of French and English literatures, and has realized that none of these literatures have existed "in isolation from the rest of the world" (p.55).

On the other hand, in the "dependent" systems, the existence and development of the literary system depends on an external system. As Even-Zohar put it "this normally occurs either when a literature is young, that is in the process of emergence, or when conditions within it have created a certain situation which cannot be dealt with by the relevant literature exclusively --or mainly --by means of its own sources" (p.55). Moreover, he believed that almost all literatures known to us have experienced such a condition in their history. In other words, "all literatures started as 'young,' and hence had to cope with conditions already generally alien to their more established contemporaries" (p.56). He added that dependence occurs in systems considered as minority literatures. According to his discussion, it is in the case of systems "which are geographically concerned to or politically subjugated by some (politically, economically) more powerful group." some examples of this introduced by Itamar Even-Zohar are Flemish vs. French, Ukrainian vs. Russian, or Norwegian vs. Danish. A shift in interference may happen, the shift from intra-literary to inter-literary interference, if minority group participates in majority system.

Itamar Even-Zohar (2010) distinguished between two types of interference, direct and indirect interferences. In the former, the interference occurs without intermediaries and the target agents can access to the source language literature. To access to the source is an easy task because they know it well. On the other hand, in the case of the indirect systems some channels takes the role of intermediary to achieve the source literature. For example, translation is considered as one channel to transfer source literature to the target literature. As stated by Even-Zohar, translation is considered as a set of texts which have been translated from a source language to the target language rather than the general activity of translating. Furthermore, he questioned the degree of exposure of the target to the source and claimed that the interference is not a matter of individual speakers.

He reasoned that "in a great number of transfer cases, acceptance or rejection of a certain item from an external source is not necessarily linked to its origin, but rather to the position it has managed to acquire within the target" (1990, p.58). Massive exposure, as Even-Zohar (2010) discussed, is one important factor that supports the impact of interference. "But such an exposure per se is neither a sufficient nor a necessary condition for interference to take place." Those minority groups that physically live among majority groups bear more influence from the massive exposure. However, he highlighted that for interference to take place, this exposure should not be considered as sufficient or a necessary condition (pp. 53-54).

2.3.1. Laws of Interference

In his seminal publication (2010), Itamar even-Zohar developed a set of laws which he believed to be governing laws with various degrees of validity of interference. Generally, he put forth three groups of aspects:

General principles of interference

1. Interference is always imminent.

2. Interference is mostly unilateral.

3. Interference may be restricted to certain domains.

Conditions for the emergence and occurrence of interference

4. Contacts will sooner or later generate interference if no resisting conditions arise.

5. Interference occurs when a system is in need of items unavailable within its own repertoire.

6. A source literature is selected by prestige.

7. A source literature is selected by dominance.

Processes and procedures of interference

8. Contacts may take place with only one part of the target literature; it may then proceed to other parts.

9. An appropriated repertoire does not necessarily maintain source literature functions.

The followings are short definition of the above hypotheses.

General Principles of Interference

No.1. Interference is always imminent.

Even-Zohar (2010) has interpreted that due to the research, interference has probably had a prominent role in the emergence of all the literary systems known to us. He held that in general, every single literature in its emergence has undergone the impact of other literatures and developed through interference. As a result, if a researcher tends to work on an unclear literature, that is whether the system has developed through interference or through its own spheres, priority ought to be given to the interference hypothesis. He reasoned that "there is not one single culture which did not emerge through interference with a more established culture; and no culture could emerge without interference at one time or another during its history" (p.55).

No. 2.Interference is mostly unilateral.

"There is no symmetry in literary interference. A target literature is, more often than not, interfered with by a source literature which may ignore it." According to Even-Zohar interference in one direction may be minor while in the other major (p.58).

No. 3.Interference may be restricted to certain domains.

Communities geographically contiguous or mixed, or otherwise linked bring forward the opinion that interference can happen not only unnecessarily on the level of literature but also on variety of levels in one system. However, providing evidence for cases when other sectors of culture remained intact and interference influenced literature only seems hard. In one word, "literary interference may be part of some wider interference processes. When this is the case, a target community may appropriate political and economic patterns, as well as social habits and cultural items" (Even-Zohar, p.62-63).

Elsewhere, Even-Zohar (2010) claimed that "a culture is never exposed to the totality of some source, even when geographically close to it or mixed with it" (p.59).

26

Conditions for the emergence and occurrence of interference

No. 4.Contacts will sooner or later generate interference if no resisting conditions arise.

Even-Zohar (2010) has stated the despite the fact that some communities live side by side one should not think that this situation necessarily generate interference. Communities can have contacts, even mix with one another, but not bring forth any interference. On the other hand, this durable contact can facilitate interference by generating conditions of availability. According to him, in some communities with highly nationalistic attitudes interference is rejected as a threat to their national integrity, while in some other societies, interference is heartily welcomed and considered good (pp.59-60). He has also debated that "It is not an easy matter, however, to determine at what point we would agree that interference has taken place or not, or at least has started to take place" (p.59).But even supposing that a community can resist interference even in cases of unavoidable contacts, it is not likely to be sure it can resist it on all levels of its system.

No.5.Interference occurs when a system is in need of items unavailable within its own repertoire.

One of the conditions for interference, according to Even-Zohar (2010, pp.62-63), is when the norms governing a system are considered by the new generation no longer effective and needed to be replaced by new ones. Interference happens when in the domestic system one cannot find proper options and he finds them in an adjacent system, thus, he gets use of them.

No.6. a source literature is selected by prestige.

Even-Zohar has stated that "a literature may be selected as a source literature because it is considered a model to emulate" (2010, p.63). Elsewhere, He had stated that "in cases of partially developed systems and minority cultures, a prestigious literature

27

may function as a literary *superstratum* for a target literature" (1990, p.66). According to him, for a literature which has not a chance to develop its own repertoire, an established literature may turn to be prestigious.

No.7. a source literature is selected by dominance.

Dominance of a system can make it to be selected as a source literature. "Naturally, a dominant literature often has prestige, but the dominant position does not necessarily result from this prestige." Even-Zohar has added that "a current case in this category is a literature made 'unavoidable' by a colonial power, which imposes its language and texts on a subjugated community"(2010, p.66). According to him (2010), most minority groups undergo such a situation. Furthermore, He claimed that interference can be consequently engendered in case of power dominance, i.e., power dominance of the imperialistic kind. Any rejecting mechanism might not be developed in cases of not-yet-established literatures, however.

Processes and procedures of interference

No.8. Contacts may take place with only one part of the target literature; it may then proceed to other parts.

"Even when appropriations are 'heavy,' there is not necessarily an overall interference. Usually certain sections remain untouched, while others undergo massive invasion, or are literally created by appropriations" (Even-Zohar, 2010, p.67). Accordingly, one stratum may be the home of interference, while other strata remain intact. Interference can move from one stratum, center, over to other one, periphery. In traditional literary studies interference has been understood in terms of "influence" which was a difference between "superiority" vs. "inferiority", therefore, one might not consider the influencing party less sophisticated than the influenced one. Even-Zohar discussed that "many peripheral literatures appropriate features of commonly accepted literary repertoire (such as 'Realism,' 'Romanticism,' 'Symbolism') after these are well established in the central literatures of a time" (p.67).

No.9. An appropriated repertoire does not necessarily maintain source literature functions.

As Itamar Even-Zohar (2010) has discussed, items existing in a source literature may assume a different function within the target literature. Any target literature appropriates items from a source literature to institutionalize itself in the first instance. Moreover, the later-generated products in any target literature compared with those that have institutionalized the literature are in all probability of a secondary nature. He added that:

This implies that a target literature frequently ignores the contemporary elements of a source literature and goes back to an earlier diachronic phase, often outdated from the point of view of the center of the *source* literature. (p.68)

The present stage of interference theory, according to Even-Zohar, does not seem capable to determine under what conditions an outdated or a novel repertoire in the source literature is appropriated by the target. In addition, for members of a minority group acquiring knowledge of a source literature tends to be more in a traditional way than the contemporary one (pp.68-69).

2.4. Review of the works on similar situations within polysystem theory

2.4.1 Interference of the Hebrew Language in Translations from Modern Hebrew Literature into Arabic

In his article, Mahmoud Kayyal (2008) assessed the linguistic interference of Hebrew on the Arabic language in general, and in Israel in particular. Thereafter, he considered the relationship between interference in general and the interference that

29

appears in translation from Modern Hebrew literature into Arabic. To achieve his purpose he has used Gideon Toury's laws of interference. Toury (1995) has put forth a number of suggestions for the formulation of law of interference:

a. In order to ensure that no interference appears in a translation, special condition and a special effort on the part of the translator are required.

b. Interference is expressed in two ways: 'negative transfer' (derivations from the rules and norms of the target system) or 'positive transfer' (the choice of linguistic forms and constructions already existing in the target language).

c. Interference is influenced by the mental and cognitive processes involved in the act of translation, in the course of which there takes place what Toury (1986: 81-83) calls 'discourse transfer' (that is to say, the source text 'imposes itself' on the translator).

d. There is a clear connection between linguistic interference and the translator's tendency to relate to the source text as a collection of small and/or low-level units rather than as a complete entity.

e. The greater the consideration for the nature of the source text when the translation is being formulated, the more interference there will be, unless the translators are particularly talented.

f. Socio-cultural factors may influence the degree of tolerance of interference. Such tolerance will tend to be greater when the translation is from a particularly prestigious culture and language, or from a 'majority' language, especially if the target language or culture is 'weak or belongs to a minority. However, the degree of tolerance of interference will not necessarily be identical on all textual an linguistic levels in the target system.

Kayyal believed that "a good deal of research has shown that interference of Hebrew in the Arabic spoken in Israel is widespread" (p.36). The researcher has studied the translations and translators of 1950s, 60s, 70s, and 80s. Accordingly, he has claimed that in 1950s and 1960s most of the translators were Jews. Although these translators were born in Arab countries, they saw themselves as belonging to Hebrew culture. This could increase the interference of Hebrew language in Arabic but "they [translators] leaned towards the extreme of acceptability, and it was this inclination, apparently, that limited interference in their work" (p.37). The article is developed through some sample translations in source language, target language and English language. Kayyal (2008, pp. 40-41) has studied these translations and concluded that there are two main reasons for the increased number of interferences in the work of translators in 1970s and 1980s:

a. The increased tendency towards adequacy in translation and towards working in small units.

b. The steadily growing penetration of Hebrew into different strata of the Arabic language, and particularly of the spoken tongue of the Arab population of Israel.

Also, he put forth a number of ways in which the interference of Hebrew in the translations of these years has expressed itself (p.41):

a. Deviation from the norms and linguistic rules of the Arabic Language.

b. Preservation of Hebrew syntactic constructions.

c. Semantic loan translations and neologisms.

d. Use of Hebrew words in Arabic translation.

e. Use of words phonetically similar to those in the original utterance.

However, the interference of the Hebrew language translations into Arabic language in Arab world has become limited. Kayyal has discovered two reasons for this, one is that "Hebrew is a minority language," the other is that there is an "ongoing Israeli-Arab conflict". He believed that the lack of interference stems from a number of causes (p.45):

31

a. Unlike the situation in Israel, in the Arab world there is no general interference of Hebrew in the Arabic language, since, as a result of the ongoing conflict, there is no direct contact between the two cultures.

b. The fact that the translators do not have a good command of the Hebrew language, and their tendency to use the translated texts in order to prove their case against Israeli society and Zionist ideology have led them to prefer to process larger units of text. When this approach is used, the possibility of interference is lower.

c. In several instances translators have used mediating translations in English. In such cases it is likely that any interference will be from English rather than (the original) Hebrew.

In short, the article studied the translations of 1950s, 60s, 70s, and 80s. In the translations of 1950s and 1960s the interference was limited, while in 1970s and 1980s it became more frequent. "On the other hand, in the translations which appeared in the Arab world... interference has been extremely limited." Kayyal concluded that this limitation was as a result of lack of "close contacts between translators and the source language, and that these contacts were sometimes limited" (p.47).

2.4.2. When a Turning Occurs: Counter-evidence to Polysytem Hypothesis

Wang Dongfeng (2008) has developed his article through Even-Zohar's polysystem hypothesis. He summarized that polysystem hypothesis suggests that "the position of the target culture that is weaker or stronger than the source culture may influence the translator's choice of translation strategies..." (p.140). According to Even-Zohar, as it is paraphrased in this article, when a translator from a weak culture translates a text from a strong culture, his or her strategy tends to be foreignisation-oriented; if otherwise, domestication-oriented. There is also convincing evidence in Israel. The writer of the article has challenged this notion and introduced counter-evidence during a certain period in China. Elsewhere, he has stated that "if a literary culture is strong enough to keep the translated literature in a secondary position, the translator tends to adopt domesticating or naturalising methods; otherwise, the translation strategy is foreignisation-oriented" (p.142).

However, Dongfeng (2008) disclaimed that in the case of Israel, a smaller or a younger culture, the situation is quite different. According to him, as Israel has a short history and its population is "so closely related to foreign cultures," its cultural identity is subject to change (p.142).

Polysystem hypothesis is a good means to study the position of Chinese culture and Chinese translators' strategic selection. In a culture like Chinese culture which has experienced a historical turning, "the position of the target culture, recognized subjectively rather than objectively by the translator, plays a more important part in determining the strategic orientation of the translation" (p.144). He added that if these two aspects, i.e., an objective position of culture and subjective recognition of culture in the translator's consciousness, are in concordance, "the translator's strategic selection operates as the polysytem hypothesis assumes," if otherwise, when discordance occurs, he has questioned (p.144), "will the translator still select his/her translation strategy as assumed in the polysystem theory?"

In the history of China, Dongfeng has introduced (2008, pp.145-150), there are four translation booms. These booms were accompanied by four turning points:

1. The translation of the Buddhist scriptures from roughly 146 to 1111.
2. The translation from the late Ming Dynasty in the early 17th century.
3. The translation from the First Opium War (1840-1842) in the late Qing Dynasty to the early years of the Republic of China in the 1920s-1930s.
4. The translation from 1978 to the present.

1. The translation of the Buddhist scriptures from roughly 146 to 1111.

In this period the culture developed more and reached its summit in Tang Dynasty. These years were along with the change from foreignisation to domestication. This change is accorded with polysytem hypothesis. Therefore, "this is a case in which the objective position of the target culture is in concordance with the translator's subjective recognition of the culture" (p.145).

2. The translation from the late Ming Dynasty in the early 17th century.

This period was accompanied by the introduction of Western science and technology. This led to the dominance of technical translation. As translations of this period are characterized by non-literary strategy, this cannot be subject of study for polysystem theory.

3. The translation from the First Opium War (1840-1842) in the late Qing Dynasty to the early years of the Republic of China in the 1920s-1930s.

Historically speaking, this boom is considered as "the great turning point from feudalism to a more democratic form of government in Chinese history, and some ways this turning is still some distance from completion" (p.146). People of this age believed that they had the most powerful nation in the world and hence they were the center of world culture. According to Dongfeng, translation in this culture "assumed the secondary position in the polysytem of the Chinese literature", while the Chinese literature in comparison with that of the Western was weaker. "Interestingly enough, as the whole culture began 'turning,' the intellectuals refused to see this weakness and resisted the turning as well" (2008, p.146). Dongfeng in this article has studied a number of translation samples to determine whether they are foreignised or domesticated translations. As a result, he found that "Chinese culture at that time witnessed foreignised translation on the one hand and domesticated ones on the other" (p.148). Accordingly, this can show that the translators' attitude towards the position of their culture plays a key role in strategic selection. He claimed that two orientations to select a specific strategy to translate a text, as introduced in polysystem hypothesis, can co-exist in a single cultural period. For another reason, such a possibility is neglected in polysytem hypothesis. According to this hypothesis, as stated before, "there is only one objective position of a culture, weak or strong, or one objective position of translated literature, primary or secondary, and hence one overall orientation of translation strategy, either foreignisation or domestication" (p.150).

The counter-evidence introduced by Wang Dongfeng (2008) is that during this historical period these two strategies co-existed, a probability "which does not necessarily undermine the base of this insightful hypothesis, but rather points to a limitation of this theory, which fails to take into account the translators' cultural psychology" (p150).

4. The translation from 1978 to the present.

In his article, Dongfeng has stated that the fourth translation boom in China is "actually the continuation of the 'turn' from feudalism to democratism..." (p.150). He believed that the situation, i.e., socio-cultural context of translation, is more complicated. On the one hand, translators use the theoretical discussions of the nature and criteria of translation discussed in the time of Yan Fu, and on the other hand, Western linguistic, philosophical and cultural, literary and translation theories have become a source for these translators (Dongfeng, 2008). Dongfeng introduced two groups in China, namely; Westernization School and School of Chinese National Culture. According to him, the former group questioned the traditional values of their culture, while the latter group believed that the have the best culture in the world except for science and technology. Consequently, this has led to a situation where, the School of Chinese National Culture, those who introduced their culture as the best one, take translation as a secondary and marginal activity, while the Westernization School do the opposite (2008, p.151). Finally, Dongfeng has concluded that the translators' attitudes toward their culture may differ, and this difference can lead to two different orientations of strategic selection.

The contribution the polysystem hypothesis makes to contemporary translation studies is that it offers a new perspective and uncovers a new factor in accounting for the adoption of different translation strategies. But, as we have seen, this hypothesis is not without limitations. In accounting for the translator's strategic selection, we have to take into consideration not only the objective position of the target culture, but also the translator's attitude towards it. Both factors can influence the translator's strategic selection. (Dongfeng, 2008, p.154)

2.4.3. The Selection of Texts for Translation in Postwar Japan, an Examination of One Aspect of Polysystem Theory

Noriko Matsunaga-Watson (2005) in his paper studied selection of texts in postwar Japan. To do so, he used polysystem as his framework and studied patterns of Japanese cultural imports. The source languages, genres and authors are the subject of this study. The scope of the paper covers the bestseller works in Japan's Publishers' yearbook 出版 年鑑. The post-Occupation (since 1952) has been subject to study the dynamics of the postwar bestseller market. Accordingly, the paper covers both fiction and non-fiction works to obtain a good grasp of the dynamics of Japan's polysystem. As he added, examining the validity of polysystem theory's views on text selection in Japan is the objective of this paper (p.161).

Polysystem theory has been used as the theoretical framework of this study. According to Even-Zohar, as Matsunaga-Watson stated, translations will take place when one or more of the following conditions are met (p.162):

1. When the polysystem of the target culture is not yet established;

2. When the polysystem of the target culture is peripheral or weak;

3. When the polysystem of the target culture is at a crisis or turning point.

"Even-Zohar also hypothesizes that texts are selected for translation for the following reasons: the prestige of the source language text, and/or the dominance of the source culture" (1990b, pp.66-68, cited in Matsunaga-Watson, 2005).

In this article, the applicability of the above hypotheses regarding the emergence of translation and text selection in postwar Japan has been examined. Moreover, other possible explanations for the emergence of translation and text selection in Japan's polysystem have been scrutinized. Matsunaga-Watson assumed that "in the case of bestseller translations in Japan's post-Occupation period, it seems that the target culture is actively seeking palatable products that satisfy the audience" (p.162). The article is developed and analyzed trough several tables and statistics. However, we attempted to summarize this article and excluded these tables.

He has analyzed that the literary polysystem of Japan of 1950s "was still largely influenced by the European macro polysystem" (p.170). He added that the result of such an influence on Japan's literary polysystem led to the selection of literary masterpieces to be translated. Furthermore, the major ground for text selection in Japan's polysystem has appeared to be due to the dominance of the source culture and the prestige of the source text (Matsunaga-Watson, 2005, p.171).

Moreover, he has claimed that the economic improvements in Japan have caused its literary polysystem to be more influenced by other polysystems, i.e., American polysystem. He claimed that " the longer interaction he selection occurs between two polysystems the more a common ground can be created" (p.171). The international market, as Matsunaga-Watson stated, is one influential factor in the selection of texts for translation in Japan. Also, elsewhere, he has written that "Japan's polysystem has become closer to the American polysystem in the 1990s" (p172).

In conclusion, Matsunaga-Watson claimed that "translation may emerge and preserve its position once it is accepted by the audience within the polysystem." Also, he concluded that translation of fiction and non-fiction categories "seems to secure a solid position in Japanese polysystem"(p.172). Two major factors of determining text selection, i.e., prestige and dominance, according to this paper, appear to be applicable to the fiction category in the early 1950s (Matsunaga-Watson, 2008, p.172). "However", he stated, "this pattern changed as time elapsed. This may be because the tastes of general audiences shifted away from such 'prestigious' works as the classics" (p.172). In the end, he has claimed that in the case of Japan's polysystem, these hypotheses are applicable.

Finally, he concluded that many factors like, commercial and other external polysystems such as politics, economics, and international relations can play a key role in text selection and the emergence of translation in Japan's polysystem.

2.4.4. Socio-Cultural Aspects of Translation into Azerbaijani in Iran: A case of a Minority Language
Ehsan Alipour (2012) in his MA dissertation has studied Azerbaijani literary system of Iran and scrutinized the position of translation within the given system, first, to study the reasons of the absence and presence of translation in Azerbaijani literary system in Iran and ,second, to describe social and cultural role of translation in the same context. He posed two sets of questions, primary and secondary questions (2012, p.5):

PQ1. Why are translations present/ absent in certain areas?

PQ2. What social and cultural roles and functions do translations play?

The secondary questions are:

SQ1. What specific areas are translations absent/present in?

SQ2. What is the degree of translation planning into Azerbaijani?

SQ3. What translation planning criteria are met in translations into Azerbaijani?

SQ4. Does translation hold a primary position or a secondary one?

In order to examine these questions, Alipour has selected Edwards' (2010) sociolinguistic framework to describe the context of Azerbaijani in Iran. He has employed González' (2005) framework of contact fields to analyze the fields in which translations were present or absent. Finally he has described the functions of translation in the context by Fouces' (2005) criteria for translation and Cronin's (1995, 1998, 2009) functions of translation. The scope of the paper is limited to the rendered translations into Azerbaijani of Iran, those that are recorded in the database of National Library. The research is both a qualitative and analytical one as it deals with defining Azerbaijani literary system as well as analyzing the causes of Azerbaijani translational situation. Alipour, in his dissertation, has attempted to explain the causes for translation as well as the functions of translation in the context of Azerbaijani literary system of Iran. To conduct his research he has prepared two sets of data (2012, p.48):

(1) Information about the eleven areas of demography, geography, economics, sociology, linguistics, psychology, history, politics-law-government, education, religion and the media [were] required by Edwards' (2010)framework ... for depicting the context of Azerbaijan and identifying the causes of translation, and (2) information about the translations rendered into Azerbaijani.

After preparing the data, he has analyzed the books and other documents to answer Edward's questions. Next, "the researcher analyzed the presence or absence of translation in different fields and subfields based on his own observations" (p.53). Afterwards, the bibliographical information of translations in terms of the categories of translation, the number of translations in 5-year periods, and the source languages and the number of translations in each were analyzed (p.53).

He concluded that Azerbaijani language is heavily dependent on Persian in many areas of life. According to him, this dependence plays "a positive role in this context" in

39

a way that Azerbaijanis struggle to maintain and preserve their language and identity (p.79). He has implied that this translational situation is "indicative of the weakness and heavy dependence of Azerbaijani on the dominant language. This leaves the language open to interference which may threat its very existence" (p.79-80). In other words, the dependence of Azerbaijani on Persian is through translation. Finally, the researcher suggested that one can study Azerbaijani of Iran from the viewpoint of linguistic aspects. Also, he recommended that studying other minority languages in Iran can be conducted within the methodological and conceptual frameworks of this study. He believed that the body of these researches "might be useful in discovering the regularities and patterns of translational behavior among different minority-language speakers" (p.80).

2.5. A review of Azerbaijani literary system

Professor Ahmet Buran and Dr. Ercan Alkaya (2009) have written that from the beginning of the 18th century, the impression of Russians had started in the region [Azerbaijan] (p.72). According to Hatice Şirin User (2006), while Ottomans and Iranians were fighting over Azerbaijan, Russians occupied Idel-Ural region; by occupying Astrakhan in 1556 they have become a neighbor of Azerbaijan. Between 1722 and 1723 Russians occupied Azerbaijan. During these years Ottomans became strong in Caucasia in the south part of Azerbaijan. In 1735, Nader Shah Afshar established his sovereignty in Iran. Iran-Russia struggles over Azerbaijan began in 1805-1813 (p.17). At the end of these struggles and according to the treaty of Turkmenchay in 1822, Azerbaijan has been divided into two regions of South and North Azerbaijan and River Aras was set as the border of these two regions (Buran & Alkaya, p. 72). Since then, according to Yavuz Akpınar (1994) the literature of the Republic of Azerbaijan is considered as "North Azerbaijani lirerarture" while the literature of Azerbaijanis in Iran is called "South Azerbaijani literature" (p.17).

40

From the linguistic geographical point of view, Azerbaijan is included of Eastern Anatolia, Northern Caucasus, Azerbaijan of Caucasus, Azerbaijan of Iran, and Iraq-Syrian Turks. After the treaty of 1828, South Azerbaijanis have used Arabic alphabet as their writing system. The center of the Azerbaijani writing system is North Azerbaijan. Today's Azerbaijani writing system is formulated of Baku, Karabakh, and Tabriz dialects triangle (Buran & Alkaya, p. 74). From the historical point of view Turks have used the following alphabets: Old Turkic, Sogut, Uyghur, Brahmi, Tibetan, Syriac, Greek, and Hebrew alphabets. Today, Latin alphabet is used in Republic of Azerbaijan, Turkmenistan, Uzbekistan, Caucasia, and Kirim population while Cyrillic alphabet is used in Kazakhstan, Kyrgyzstan and Tatarstan in Russian Federation. Generally, Turks have used the following alphabets in a large scale in their lifetime; Gokturk, Uygur, Arabic, Latin and Cyrillic (User, pp. 26-27).

Arabic alphabet had been used in North Azerbaijan until 1929. Latin alphabet was substituted with Arabic alphabet in 1922; consequently, Arabic alphabet was discarded. Between 1922 and 1929 these two alphabets were used side by side. From 1939 Cyrillic alphabet was used in North Azerbaijan. Since 1992 Latin alphabet has been used in this region and in 2001 it was approved by the government of the Republic of Azerbaijan (User cited in Buran & Ercan, p.74).

Hatice Şirin User (2006) claimed that after the Treaty of Turkmenchay in 1828, South Azerbaijanis (Azerbaijanis of Iran) were not influenced by the process of modernization in North Azerbaijan (in Russia). Consequently, they have followed classic literature and Arabic-Persian alphabet (p138). In the case of South Azerbaijani writing system, User (2006) has stated that Arabic alphabet has been the only writing system used by South Azerbaijanis from the beginning of writing. South Azerbaijanis have never had a reformation in their alphabet. Even the reformation of alphabet has not been negotiated for a long time in Iran; however, various activities have been started in

41

the reformation of this alphabet in the recent years. Today, this alphabet after the reformations is called "Turkish Alphabet" (p.142).

She also added that Turks of South Azerbaijan, like other communities that use Turkish-Arabic alphabet, have undergone an alphabetic reform in the late epoch. The reform in the alphabet had started by Mirza Fathali Akhundzadeh and Malkum Khan. But Akhundadeh's attempts to reform the alphabet were unsuccessful. However, this alphabet has been modified in 19th and 20th century in Iran. In the first and second Orthography Seminar held in Iran, this alphabet has been called as "Turkish Alphabet" (pp. 139-140).

User (2006) has claimed that South Azerbaijanis have developed press and information activities. It is believed that the press and printing industry and magazines of South Azerbaijanis in the time of Pahlavi Dynasty were more developed than North Azerbaijanis'. Between 1906 and 1911 in Iran, Shafag, Tabriz, Mukafat, Islah, Farvarzin and many other magazines were published. Molla Nasreddin magazine that began in 1906 in Tiflis started to be published in 1921 in Tabriz. The press and printing industry was established in South Azerbaijan before the Treaty of Turkmenchay. In 1817, Abbas Mirza established a stone printing house. Anjuman magazine was printed in the printing house in 1819. Seda in 1822, Anjuman II in 1856, Azerbaijan in 1858, Akhtar in 1875, Vatan in 1876, and Tabriz in 1879 are magazines and newspapers that were published in this printing house (p.139).

Süer Eker (2010) has stated that Turkish language is spread from Germany to Eastern Europe. He introduced Turkish speaking countries as: Turkey, Turkmenistan, Azerbaijan, Uzbekistan, Kirgizstan, Kazakhstan, Turkish Republic of Northern Cyprus, East Turkistan (Sinkiang), Chuvashia, Republic of Hakasya, Tatarstan, Tyva Republic, Republic of Dagestan, Bash Kurdistan, Altai Republic, Gagauzia, Kabardino-Balkar Republic, Karachay–Cherkess Republic, Afghanistan, Syria, Iraq, Islamic Republic of Iran, Greece, Albania, Tajikistan, Ukraine, Mongolia, Macedonia, Bulgaria, Yugoslavia,

Romania, Germany, and other European, American and Australian countries (p. 88). In His book, titled Çağdaş Türk Dili [contemporary Turkish Language](2010), Süer Eker has stated that 13,000,000 out of 62,000,000 of the population of Iran are Azeri, while the population of Azeri people in the Republic of Azerbaijan is 6,000,000 out of 7,500,000. On the other hand, Buran and Alkaya (2009) claimed that according to the 2002 census, population of the Republic of Azerbaijan is 8,202,500 and population of Turks in Iran is 20 million (p.77).

Professor Ahmet Buran and Dr. Ercan Alkaya (2009) has described that Azerbaijani literature is considered as the literatures of the Turks of Caucasia, North Azerbaijan (Republic of Azerbaijan), South Azerbaijan (Iran), Iraq, and Eastern Anatolia (Turkey) (p.74). They have added that between 17th and 18th century Ashik literature was presented by Poets like Kurbanî, Kürenî, Tufarkanlı Abbas, Mevcî, Hasta Kasım, and Lezgi Ahmet in the region. For the classic poetry they introduced Kavsi Tebrizî, Saib Tebrizî, Nişat Şirvanî, Ağa Mesih Şirvanîç Safî, Fazlî, Şakir, Mehcur, Molla Penah Vakıf. Among these literatures, they believed that Varka ve Gülşah, Aşık Garip, Kerem ile Aslı, and Abbas ve Gülgez are shinning and important. Moreover, in modern cultural magazines, Gülistan, Divan-ı Hikmet, Mecmua-i Şuara ve Meclis-i Üns are emphasized. Modern Poetry is presented by poets like Kasım Beg Zakir, Kutsî, Vazıh, Hurşit banu and Seyyid Azim Şirvanî. In the gneres like novel and short story, İsmail Beg Kutkaşanlı, Sultan Mecid Ganizade, Celil Memmedguluzade, Neriman Nerimanov, Süleyman Sani Ahundov, Syit Hüseyin, Eli Veliyev, Mirza İbrahimov, İlyas Efendiev, are named.Mirza Fethali Ahundzade, as they believed, is pioneer in theater and play writing (pp. 74-75).

Chapter Three:

Methodology

3.1. Overview

This chapter provides a description of the methodological framework of the research. In section 3.2, research types and methods are described. In section 3.3, the procedure of the data collection has been explained. Finally, in section 3.4, the procedure of data analysis is provided.

3.2. Design

According to Birjandi and Mosallanejad (2005) if the subject of the study deals with issues which are not directly observable, the researcher would better follow the principles of qualitative research. They defined the non-directly observable issues as "those which do not exist in the physical world" (p.182). As the present study does not exist in the physical world it overlapped with the qualitative research. Moreover, Williams and Chesterman believed that qualitative research describes the quality of the subject of study in some enlightening way. They also thought that "qualitative research can lead to conclusions about what is possible, what can happen, or what can happen at least sometimes; it doesn't allow conclusions about what is probable, general, or universal" (2002, p.64). The aim of this research is to reach to such conclusions about what is possible and what can happen. Furthermore, the study intended to apply the polysystem theory to the case of literary system of Azerbaijani in Iran in order to describe the nature as well as explain the reasons of the existence of the given system. Azerbaijani literary system in Iran was selected as a case for this study because it has been seen as a unique case which overlapped with the hypotheses of the polysystem theory. Williams and Chesterman held that "case studies can be exploratory (what can

45

we find out about X?), descriptive (what is the nature of X?) Or explanatory (why X, how X?)"(p. 65). They have introduced a set of reasons to study a case in a research. They added that "a case might be selected for study because it is seen as obviously of special interest, a unique case ...; or because it seems relevant for a fruitful comparison; or because it is entirely new and therefore interesting; or because it seems to be a critical or typical case against which a theoretical claim can be tested" (pp. 65-66). The main purpose of this study is, regarding Farhady's (2011, p.107) definition of the case study as investigation of a social unit, to investigate the laws of literary interference in the literary system of Azerbaijani in Iran. He also professed that "a case study may provide the researcher with valuable pieces of information which would make generating fruitful hypotheses possible" (p.107). In addition to the above types, this study is also a historical and library research type.

The research was primarily designed to apply Even-Zohar's (2010) laws of literary interference to Azerbaijani literature in Iran. To do so, first, it was necessary to analyze and describe this literary system, second, to gather the number of books existing in this system statistically and finally to apply laws of literary interference to the literary system of it to determine whether these laws are applicable. The information thus obtained was the basis of the researcher's interpretations of the phenomenon. Polysystem theory (2010) was chosen as the framework for analyzing the situation. This framework required analyzing the situation of Azerbaijani literary system in Iran according to the number of books, their genres, source languages, target languages, and years of publication in order to apply the laws of literary interference to this system. Internet was the primary instrument to statistically gather the number of books, their genres, source languages, target languages and the year of the publication. National Library and Archives of I.R of Iran was the source of information. No other instrument did prove to be more useful than internet to obtain bibliographical information about books published in Azerbaijani.

46

The obtained information of the books was primarily categorized into two groups of the original writings and translated books. Then, these two groups have been categorized according to their genres, source languages and target languages. Finally, these books have been categorized according to their year of publication since the Islamic revolution of Iran. This information was used to describe the situation of South Azerbaijani literary system. Therefore, findings will be based only on the provided data.

3.3. Data Collection

Data required in this research to be conducted was the number of the books in Azerbaijani literary system. To obtain this information Internet was used as the instrument of data collection. However, National library and Archives of Islamic Republic of Iran was the only source of the bibliographical information of the published books in Azerbaijani in Iran. The researcher accessed the following link on 2 November 2012: http://opac.nlai.ir/opac-prod/search/bibliographicAdvancedSearch.do;jsessionid=A2CA904079C242403977908 51FF76D39?command=NEW_SEARCH&classType=0&pageStatus=1

He searched for the word"ترکی"[=Turkic] in the "note" field. The result showed that 3,767 out of 2,174,035 books were recorded with that label. Some of them were non-book materials like magazines, CDs, Cassettes, newspapers, etc. Some other books were published in Latin or Cyrillic alphabet for the Republic of Azerbaijan or Turkey. Moreover, there were some books that were in other forms of Turkish, for example, Qashqai, Turkmen, etc. All of these books were ignored. The researcher analyzed all the records and extracted all the books that were written in Azerbaijani with Arabic alphabet. Then, these books were primarily categorized into two groups of "original books" and "translated books".

Afterward, the original books were analyzed and subsequently categorized according to their genres. This resulted in 9 groups; religion, drama, biography, history,

47

dictionary, language and linguistics, literature and folklore, poetry, and fiction. There were some books which were translated from Azerbaijani in Iran into other languages. These books also were categorized according to their target languages; Persian, English and Azerbaijani of the Republic of Azerbaijan. Next, the research needed the number of the books rendered from other languages into Azerbaijani in Iran. The researcher has analyzed the population and extracted all the translated books and categorized them according to their source languages. This has resulted in English, Arabic, Persian, Russian, Turkish, Azerbaijani of the Republic of Azerbaijan, and other. The last group, i.e., "other", included the languages that had one or two books, thus, the researcher decided to categorize them into another group and label them as "other".

Next, the group of the source languages was analyzed and every participant of the group was categorized according to its genres. Eventually, all the books in the "original books," "Translated into Azerbaijani" and "translated from Azerbaijani" were categorized according to their years of publication since the Islamic Revolution of Iran. The process was completed in 35 days.

However, there were some barriers to the easy processing of the data:

1. In some cases, the bibliographical information failed to have complete information about the book. This took more time for the researcher to determine in which group the book must be categorized. The researcher sometimes had to get information from some other sources like publication houses via internet. In the case he couldn't be sure enough, he avoided the record.

2. National Library and Archives of Iran in some databases did not prepare complete information. For example, the researcher has found some translations that their bibliography failed to indicate their source or target languages, and sometimes their genres. In such cases too, the researcher ignored the record.

3. Some books were recorded twice. After analyzing these records, the researcher decided to include them in the population because they had either different publications or different translators.

The criteria for choosing the records were works that were in Azerbaijani with Arabic alphabet, their place of publication and their publishers.

Figure 3.1 A sample record obtained via the database

3.4 Procedure of Data Analyzing

In his seminal publication (2010), Itamar Even-Zohar developed a set of laws which he believed to be governing laws with various degrees of validity of interference. Generally, he put forth three groups of aspects:

General principles of interference

1. Interference is always imminent.

2. Interference is mostly unilateral.

3. Interference may be restricted to certain domains.

Conditions for the emergence and occurrence of interference

4. Contacts will sooner or later generate interference if no resisting conditions arise.

5. Interference occurs when a system is in need of items unavailable within its own repertoire.

6. A source literature is selected by prestige.

7. A source literature is selected by dominance.

Processes and procedures of interference

8. Contacts may take place with only one part of the target literature; it may then proceed to other parts.

9. An appropriated repertoire does not necessarily maintain source literature functions.

In the first stage, the researchers selected four of these hypotheses because they found them more homogeneous and decided to put them in one group. These four hypotheses are:

1. Interference is mostly unilateral

2. Contacts will sooner or later generate interference if no resisting conditions arise.

3. Interference occurs when a system is in need of items unavailable within its own repertoire.

4. Contacts may take place with only one part of the target literature; it may then proceed to other parts.

Generally, these four hypotheses deal with the nature (what), conditions (why), and processes (how) of the literary interference. The first one, i.e., interference is mostly unilateral, deals with the nature of the literary interference in a system. According to Even-Zohar (2010) interference in a system can be either unilateral or bilateral. In other words, while interference in one direction is minor, in the other direction can be major. The data in this article will be studied to determine whether translation, an indirect literary interference, is mostly unilateral or bilateral. To do this, the number of the translated books from and into the literary system of South Azerbaijani will be studied statistically. Also, the researcher will study the years of the publications of the books to see in which year(s) interference has increased or decreased.

The second and the third selected hypotheses deal with the conditions (why) of the literary interference. These two hypotheses are;

- Contacts will sooner or later generate interference if no resisting conditions arise.
- Interference occurs when a system is in need of items unavailable within its own repertoire.

To study these hypotheses in the case of Azerbaijani literature in Iran the researchers need to study the genres of the original books to determine the presence and absence of books in each genre. Then, data obtained from studying the genres of the original books will be analyzed in comparison with genres of the translated books. This will be useful to present the existing genres of the literary system of Azerbaijani in order to see if the absence of (a) certain genre(s) is compensated by translation. Moreover, the researchers will study the reason of literary interference in this literary system. To do so, the possible resisting conditions will be studied as well.

51

The last hypothesis is mostly dealing with the processes (how) of the literary interference. Contacts may take place with only one part of the target literature; it may then proceed to other parts. In order to study this hypothesis, the year of the publications of the original and translated books as well as the genres and source languages will be analyzed. This study can provide the researchers with the data that can demonstrate whether literary interference took place with only on part of Azerbaijani literary system, and then proceed to other parts.

However, the rest of the hypotheses will be discarded in this research. Why these hypotheses are not covered in this research will be explained. In the General principles of interference, the hypotheses number 1 and 3 are discarded. Theses hypotheses are; *interference is always imminent* and *interference may be restricted to certain domains*. Because the present research is a synchronic study that is concerned with Azerbaijani literary system in a limited time period, the first hypothesis will be ignored for it is concerned with a diachronic type of study. The word "always" in this hypothesis is an evidence for the claim.

The third hypothesis is discarded, because it deals with certain domains. These domains can be political, social, power, literary, historical, cultural, and other systems. The present research attempts to consider only one domain, i.e., literary domain. To apply this hypothesis one should take into account all of these domains, such a study that cannot be covered in this research.

In the second aspect of the literary interference which is concerned with the conditions for the emergence and occurrence of interference; (6) a source literature is selected by prestige and (7) source literature is selected by dominance; are ignored in the present study, because number 6 deals with a social, cultural, or political issue and number 7 is concerned with lingual and literal problem. As the purpose of the study is to study the literary aspect of the literary system of Azerbaijani, these two hypotheses are discarded as well.

The last set of the hypotheses deals with the processes and procedures of interference. The hypothesis number (9)"an appropriated repertoire does not necessarily maintain source literature functions" is ignored, because it is concerned with a functional study. Therefore, this type of the study is not the purpose of the present research.

The following figure shows which of the hypotheses are selected and which one are avoided.

Table 3.1 Selected and avoided hypotheses in the present research

Hypotheses of the Literary Interference	Choice
1. Interference is always imminent	✗
2. Interference is mostly unilateral.	✓
3. Interference may be restricted to certain domains.	✗
4. Contacts will sooner or later generate interference if no resisting conditions arise.	✓
5. Interference occurs when a system is in need of items unavailable within its own repertoire.	✓
6. A source literature is selected by prestige.	✗
7. A source literature is selected by dominance.	✗
8. Contacts may take place with only one part of the target literature; it may then proceed to other parts.	✓
9. An appropriated repertoire does not necessarily maintain source literature functions.	✗

Chapter Four:

Data Analysis

4.1. Overview

In this chapter, the results and findings of the data analysis as well as discussions of the results are presented. In section 4.2, an introduction to the data analysis of this chapter is provided. In sections 4.3, 4.4, 4.5, and 4.6, four hypothesis of the literary interference are discussed and analyzed according to the provided data.

4.2. Data Analysis

Marta García González (2005) in her article titled "translation of minority language in bilingual and multilingual communities," has stated that "the volume of translation activity between minority languages can be an important indicator of the language status, both at the institutional and at the social level" (p.114). But she believed that such data are not sufficient if a researcher wants to study the status of a minority language in relation to a majority language. Therefore, she has added that:

However, to attain the goal of the study, that is, to work out the reasons that determine the effective practice of translation from and into minority languages, we need data apart from the incidence of translation. We would also need data concerning the present and past situation of the language, its history, its legal and social status, the fields where it is mainly used, etc. it is only by analyzing and comparing such data that we will be able to understand the real status of translation in each studied translation. (p.117)

To provide such data, she has suggested a model based on Verdoodt, Kloss and McConnell (1989) (see Table 4.1.). The below data are provided in chapter 3 as well as

55

the present chapter of this research. Accordingly, she discussed that there are three different types of language contact:

   a. Contacts between the minority language and the major dominant language

   b. Contacts between the minority language and other major languages

   c. Contacts between the minority language and other minority languages

Table4.1 Language Description Table

LANGUAGE DESCRIPTION
1. Language name(s) and main varieties
2. Relation between the language and the major language of the state
3. Language family
4. Short historical description
5. Standard variety
6. Number and nature of speakers
7. Status of the language
Legal status
Social status: speakers' attitudes towards the language
8. Language protection
9. Language and public administration
10. Private sectors
11. Language and religion
12. Literature
13. Education
Primary education
Secondary education
University education
14. Periodicals and mass media

Periodicals
Radio – TV
15. Other remarks

Therefore, the research is based on two sets of information. One is the data of the incidence of translation; the second is the historical, linguistic, and social status of Azerbaijani in Iran. Table 4.2 was first filled by Ehsan Alipour in 2012 in his Masters dissertation (p. 68). In the present research we have added to this table as much information as was obtained. The following figure describes the translation status of Azerbaijani of Iran in relation to the dominant major language, other major languages and other minor languages.

In the following paragraphs, the researchers have studied and analyzed four hypotheses of Even-Zohar (2010) in the case of literary system of Azerbaijani of Iran. The research is developed based on the provided data and Even-Zohar's (2010) laws of literary interference.

Key to table:

A: Translations between the minority and the national language

B: Translation between the minority and other major languages

C: Translations between the minority and other minority languages

√/x/?: There is translation / there is no translation / I do not know

No.: Amount of translations (in percentages / number / frequency (very often /often / sometimes / rarely / never)

Table 4.2 Language Description Tables of Azerbaijani of Iran

FIELDS	SUB-FIELDS	A (MinL/MajL) √/x/? No.	B (MinL/OMajL) √/x/? No.	C (MinL/OM inL) √/x/? No.
1.PUBLIC SCOPE				
Government	Executive work	?	?	?
Legislative	Legislation	?	?	?
	Chamber meetings	?	?	?
Judicial	Legal procedures	?	?	?
	Legal documents	?	?	?
Public Administration	Administrative documentation	?	?	?
International Relations	International legislation	?	?	?
	Meetings	?	?	?
2. MIXED SCOPE- PUBLIC/PRIVATE				
Culture and	Textbooks	x	x	x
Education	Research	?	?	?
	Conferences	?	?	?
The Media	News agencies	√ always	x	x
	Interviews (TV/papers)	?	x	x

58

	Series/Films/Documentaries	√1	?	x
3. PRIVATE SCOPE				
Publishing industry	Literature	√ 54	√ 231	√ 1
	Linguistic texts	x	√ 4	x
	Dictionary	x	√ 1	x
	Folklore texts	√ 6	√ 52	x
	Religious texts	√ 12	√ 43	x
	Biography	√ 8	√ 5	x
	Political texts	√ 4	x	x
Private business sector	Production	?	?	?
	Business Relations	?	?	?
	Advertising Labeling	?	?	?
Film Industry	Films	?	?	?
	Independent Films	?	?	?

4.3. Interference is Mostly Unilateral

Even-Zohar (2010) believed that "there is no symmetry in cultural contacts." By this he meant that a target culture is interfered with by a source culture and this interference is mostly unilateral. In other words, when there is interference between two cultures, this interference is not balanced. To analyze this hypothesis in the case of Azerbaijani literary system in Iran, two sets of data were prepared. The first set of data was the number of the imported and exported books in Azerbaijani literature in Iran. The second set of data is the number of imported and exported books by their source and target languages.

According to Figure 4.1, the number of the translated books into Azerbaijani was 468, whereas the number of the translated books from this language into other languages was 86. From the following figure it was evident that translation into Azerbaijani of Iran has been more than translation from it.

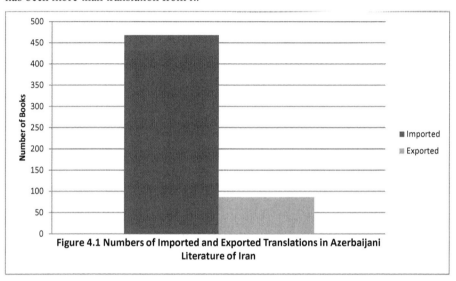

Figure 4.1 Numbers of Imported and Exported Translations in Azerbaijani Literature of Iran

In order to determine that what languages have been selected as the source language, the number of the imported books by their source languages have been prepared. In addition to this set of data, the number of the exported books by their target languages was put alogside.

Figure 4.2 indicates that Azerbaijani in Iran has translated books rather from the Azerbaijani of the Republic of Azerbaijan and Persian than other source languages. The number of the translations from the Republic of Azerbaijan was 244, whereas the number of the books translated into this language from Azerbaijani in Iran was 4. There

60

were 87 records for Persian as the source language. On the other hand, the number of the translated books from Azerbaijani literature in Iran into Persian was 73.

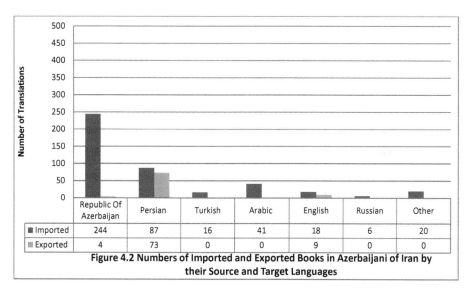

	Republic Of Azerbaijan	Persian	Turkish	Arabic	English	Russian	Other
Imported	244	87	16	41	18	6	20
Exported	4	73	0	0	9	0	0

Figure 4.2 Numbers of Imported and Exported Books in Azerbaijani of Iran by their Source and Target Languages

Even-Zohar (2010) has hypothesized that "interference is mostly unilateral." In other words, when there is interference between two cultures, "there may be some minor interference in one direction and a major one in another" (p.58). He has introduced two types of interference, namely; direct and indirect. By the first type he meant that "a source literature is available to, and accessed by, agent of the target literature without intermediaries." In the second type, according to him, "interference is intermediated through some channel, such as translation" (1990, p.57). The provided data showed that there were contacts between the literary system of Azerbaijani in Iran and other source languages. Among the translations, translation from the Republic of Azerbaijan seemed to be significant, because the number of the imported books was more than the exported texts. It is evident that, according to the provided data, the number of the imported

61

translations from the Republic of Azerbaijan has been more than the number of the exported books to this language.

In whole, the data showed that the imported translations were more in comparison to the number of exported texts. What seems important in the case of the Azerbaijani of the Republic of Azerbaijan is that this language has played a key role as the literary source for Azerbaijani of Iran. The following table shows that how the Azerbaijani of the Republic of Azerbaijan has been increasingly selected as the source for translation by the literary system of Azerbaijani in Iran over time.

What has been discussed so far is the number of the contacts between the literary system of Azerbaijani in Iran and other literary systems. Even-Zohar (2010) believed that "it is not an easy matter, however, to determine at what point we would agree that interference has started to take place" (p.59). Therefore, to determine at what point the literary system of Azerbaijani in Iran has been interfered with by other literatures seems to be a difficult matter. Even-Zohar (2010) discussed that the exchange of goods is one of manifestations of contacts. Due to him, these goods, whether they have been imported unilaterally or multilaterally, may become important items in the culture of the importing society (2010). He has also claimed that durable contacts will facilitate interference; therefore, he stated that "durable contacts, while not producing conspicuously visible interference, may, however, generate conditions of availability, which will facilitate interference" (2010, pp. 59-60).

Accordingly, the trends of imported and exported translations in the literary system of Azerbaijani literature in Iran have been provided over time. Figure 4.3[1] showed that in the course of time, the number of imported translations is more in comparison to the number of exported translations in the literary system of Azerbaijani of Iran. This is evident that there are durable contacts between the literary system of Azerbaijani of Iran

---

[1] The dates of the tables are in the solar year. In order to change them into the Christian year add 621 to each year. For example; 1357+621=1978 AC

and other literary systems. The following figure showed that interference in the case of literary system of Azerbaijani of Iran is unilateral.

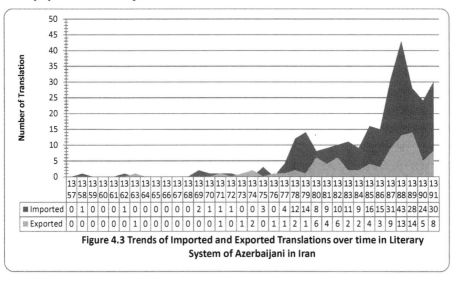

	13 57	13 58	13 59	13 60	13 61	13 62	13 63	13 64	13 65	13 66	13 67	13 68	13 69	13 70	13 71	13 72	13 73	13 74	13 75	13 76	13 77	13 78	13 79	13 80	13 81	13 82	13 83	13 84	13 85	13 86	13 87	13 88	13 89	13 90	13 91
■ Imported	0	1	0	0	0	1	0	0	0	0	0	0	2	1	1	1	0	0	3	0	4	12	14	8	9	10	11	9	16	15	31	43	28	24	30
▦ Exported	0	0	0	0	0	0	1	0	0	0	0	0	0	0	1	0	1	2	0	1	1	2	1	6	4	6	2	2	4	3	9	13	14	5	8

Figure 4.3 Trends of Imported and Exported Translations over time in Literary System of Azerbaijani in Iran

4.4. Contacts will sooner or later generate interference if no resisting conditions arise.

Even-Zohar (2010) has doubted whether "contacts are sooner or later likely to generate some kind of interference" (p.61). In other words, it's not for sure to claim that every possible contact will generate interference, because in some highly nationalistic societies interference is rejected, whereas in other societies everything coming from abroad is treated as good (Even-Zohar, 2010). However, he added that "if one argues that such interference could have taken place because of some kind of vacuum, indifference, or lack of resistance in the target- that would amount to the same hypothesis" (2010, p.61). By this, he meant that if one wants to study the interference within a society, he/she needs to take into account the possible vacuums, indifferences, or lack of resistance. Therefore, in the case of literary system of Azerbaijani in Iran these items needed to be studied in order to determine whether contacts have generated interference. To do so, we needed two sets of data. Firstly, the linguistic-geographical as well as historical condition of Azerbaijani in Iran; secondly, the trend of translations from Azerbaijani of the Republic of Azerbaijan and Persian over the time were studied.

4.4.1. linguistic-geographical and historical condition of Azerbaijani in Iran
According to the Administrative Department of the President of the Republic of Azerbaijan:

> A war between Iran and Russia resulted in signing two agreements [of] Gulustan (1818), Turkmenchay (1827) which divided Azerbaijan in two parts. Thus, for nearly 200 years, two parts of one nation live separately and in quite different conditions and environment.

> Like other spheres, the difference lies also in literary language. The language of independent Azerbaijan still contains traces of Russian language, while the language of South Azerbaijan [Azerbaijani of Iran] is influenced by the Persian language. At present, literary language of North and South Azerbaijan still differ in vocabulary, phonetics and in some way grammar (especially, in syntax). (p.8)

Moreover, the paper has emphasized that the different Turkish languages residing in different countries have been much influenced by the literary language of the Republic of Azerbaijan and consequently, they have attempted to draw closer to this literary language. After the Treaties of Turkmenchay and Gulustan, according to Yavuz Akpınar (1994), the literature of the Republic of Azerbaijan is considered as "North Azerbaijani literature" while the literature of Azerbaijanis in Iran is called "South Azerbaijani literature" (p.17).

Since the Islamic Revolution of Iran in 1979 Azerbaijanis of Iran have continued producing texts in their literature like before. In addition, they have translated several texts from various source languages. Among other languages, like Arabic that is a source of religious texts for Azerbaijanis, it is evident that the literatures of Iran and Republic of Azerbaijan have played a key role in the formation of Azerbaijani repertoire in Iran. For Persian, it is the official language and consequently seems to have a major direct impact on the given literature. On the other hand, the literature of the Republic of Azerbaijan has become a source of text importation for Azerbaijani in Iran.

4.4.2. The position of translation in the literary system of Azerbaijani in Iran

Translation from the literature of the Republic of Azerbaijan into Azerbaijani in Iran is called as "کوچورمه," "kochurme" [=Köçürmə].Translation from the literature of the Republic of Azerbaijan into Azerbaijani of Iran is known as "*Kochurme.*". This seems to be a unique type of translation that occurs between two Turkic family languages, for example; Turkish-Azerbaijani translations. It is possible to think of the term "transliterate" as an alternative term for this type of translation by now. Changing the alphabet from Latin to Arabic and keeping as much style of the source as possible, in case of translation from the literature of the Republic of Azerbaijan into the literature of Azerbaijani of Iran and vice versa, seems to be the main change in this type of translation.

Therefore, all translations from the literature of the Republic of Azerbaijan or Turkey into the literature of Azerbaijani in Iran are called as "kochurme." The following figure is a sample title page of a translated book from the Republic of Azerbaijan. According to the Figure 4.4, the person who has rendered the text is called as "کوچورون," which means the doer of *kochurme*.

65

سرشناسه	:	حسین، توفیق
عنوان و نام پدیدآور	:	سنین یاخشیلیغین (شعرلر و پوئمالار)/ توفیق حسین؛ کوچورون داود یوسف‌پور.
مشخصات نشر	:	تهران: اندیشه نو، ۱۳۸۸.
مشخصات ظاهری	:	۱۳۹ص.
شابک	:	۹۷۸-۹۶۴-۹۱٤۹-٦۱٤-۷۴-۸
وضعیت فهرست نویسی	:	فیپا
یادداشت	:	ترکی.
یادداشت	:	واژه‌نامه.
موضوع	:	شعر ترکی -- جمهوری آذربایجان -- قرن ۲۰م.
شناسه افزوده	:	یوسف‌پور، داود، مترجم
رده بندی کنگره	:	PL۳۱۴/ح۵۲۴۳س۹۱۳۸۸
رده بندی دیویی	:	۳۶۱۱/۸۹۴
شماره کتابشناسی ملی	:	۲۳۳۴۲۹۱

(سنین یاخشیلیغین (شعرلر و پوئمالار) آدرس ثابت

Figure 4.4A Sample Title Page of a Translated Book from the Republic of Azerbaijan

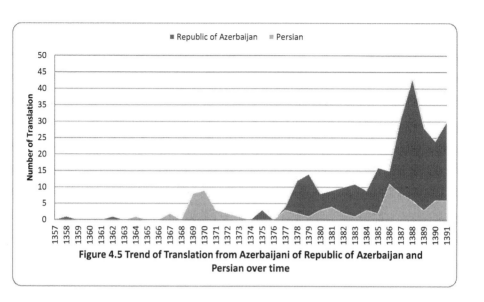

Figure 4.5 Trend of Translation from Azerbaijani of Republic of Azerbaijan and Persian over time

In the recent years, especially since 1376 the number of this type of translation has been increasing according to the figure 4.5. The occurrence of the phenomenon i.e., *Kochurme*, could have not only linguistic but also literary and political reasons. The linguistic condition could deal with the grammatical, semantic and syntactic shifts in the process of the translation, whereas the literary and political condition of this type of translation could be traced back in the historical conditions of the two regions. What seems important here is that the utmost number of translations from other languages into the Azerbaijani of Iran belonged to the category of the Republic of Azerbaijan. Thus, it seems that in the light of the indirect literary interference *Kochurme* plays an important role. The occurrence of this type of translation could have linguistic and literary reasons as well. As the language in the Republic of Azerbaijan and Azerbaijan of Iran is the same, with slight differences and different alphabetic systems, as well as their geographical and cultural background, it is evident that translating from a source

67

repertoire of the Republic of Azerbaijan seems more justified than translating from far different languages.

According to Nam Fung Chang (2011,p.315) 'If Literature A translates less from Literature B than vice versa, that would be one of the manifestations of the centrality of Literature A in relation to Literature B.' Therefore, if the literature of the Republic of Azerbaijan is considered as Literature A and the literature of Azerbaijan of Iran is Literature B, and if we consider the number of translations between these two languages, it would be one of the manifestations of the centrality of literature of the Republic of Azerbaijan in relation to the literature of Azerbaijan of Iran. Figure 4.6 indicated that the number of the translations from Literature A into B is more than vice versa.

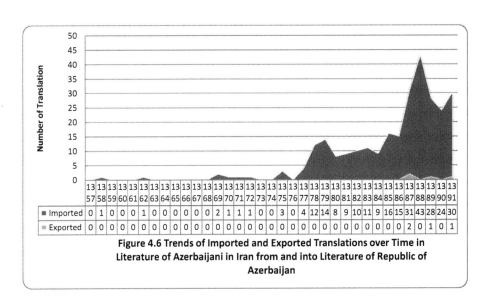

Figure 4.6 Trends of Imported and Exported Translations over Time in Literature of Azerbaijani in Iran from and into Literature of Republic of Azerbaijan

In addition, Yahalom (1979, p.65, translated by Codde, 2003, p.114, cited in Nam Fung Chang 2011) has pointed out that "when a system imports from a neighboring system, the home system will consider the adjacent system 'more "complete," "developed," or "adapted" for the attainment of a certain goal, while considering itself 'inferior'" (p.317). Therefore, according to the above discussion as well as the data provided in figure4.6, resistance against translation from Persian literary system is evident which manifests itself as tendency towards importing translation from the literature of the Republic of Azerbaijan. Such translations are called *Kochurme*.

Figure 4.5 indicates that the number of the translations from the repertoire of the Republic of Azerbaijan has been more in comparison to that of Persian's. According to the figure 4.6, the number of the texts imported from the Republic of Azerbaijan has increasingly heightened in the recent years. Year 1376 seems to be a turning point in translation for Azerbaijani of Iran, because the translations form these two languages have gradually increased over time.

Marta García González (2005) claims that the purpose of translation in the case of minority languages is language recovery or preservation.

In the case of minority languages, on the contrary, translation is an activity that has to be fostered and activated, as a mechanism to promote the language itself. In other words, translation is no longer an underlying element of communication, but an essential tool in the process of language recovery or preservation, and therefore it is more likely to be studied in relation to language and culture planning than translation between major languages. (p.111)

Consequently, we face the question of whether translation, especially *Kochurme*, has played as a tool in the process of recovery and preservation of Azerbaijani of Iran. According to the above discussions, it seems that this language in the process of its recovery and preservation has mostly relied on the literature of the Republic of Azerbaijan rather than other languages. On the other hand, Persian as the official language of the country has played a major role in the life of this language. In

69

conclusion, although Azerbaijani in Iran is highly dependent to Persian in the areas like education, the literature of the Republic of Azerbaijan seems to be a reliable source for translation and consequently preservation of this literature.

4.5. Interference occurs when a system is in need of items unavailable within its own repertoire.

In order to study this hypothesis, two sets of data were required. Firstly, it was needed to determine what items were available within the repertoire of Azerbaijani of Iran to judge what items were needed to be imported. Secondly, the imported translations needed to be categorized by their genres to decide whether the unavailability of an item in the repertoire has been provided through translation. The following figure shows the two sets of data side by side.

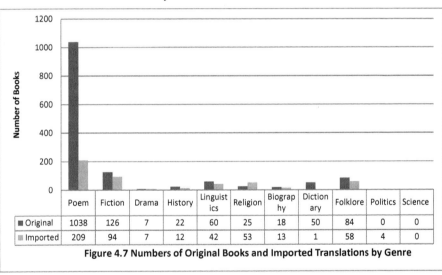

Figure 4.7 Numbers of Original Books and Imported Translations by Genre

Figure 4.7 demonstrated that there were 9 main categories within the repertoire of Azerbaijani in Iran; poem, fiction, drama, history, linguistics, religion, biography,

70

dictionary, and folklore. The utmost number of original genre belonged to poem with 1038 records. Next, fiction, folklore, linguistics, and dictionary categories were 126, 84, 60, and 50 respectively. Other categories, like religion, history, biography, and drama had the least amount. However, in the categories of "politics" and "science" no item was recorded.

According to the provided data, Azerbaijani literature in Iran has imported the items that were available within itself. For example, the categories of "poem," "fiction" and "folklore" that were available within the repertoire have been imported through translation. Other items have undergone the same process. Only 4 political books were translated into the repertoire. The category of "science" was not recorded in the repertoire. In spite of the fact that the unavailable items within the repertoire were not provided through translation, one should not jump to conclusions and think that this hypothesis is disproved.

Considering the linguistic condition of Azerbaijanis in Iran could be helpful. Persian is the official language of the country; therefore, scientific, academic and literal texts are produced in this language. Azerbaijanis, like other minorities in Iran, study Persian language at schools and universities. Scientific texts are also written in Persian which is the official language. So, Azerbaijanis in Iran might have not been in need of scientific items in their own language, because these items were already available within the repertoire of Persian, a language they can read and speak, therefore, no translation has been recorded in this field.

On the other hand, this case can be discussed from the viewpoint of politics and power relations. Alexandra Jaffe (2010) in her paper "Locating powers: Corsican translators and their critics" has offered the term "diglossia," by this, she meant that a minority language may be excluded from the powerful public sphere and consequently relegate to informal and family domains. Similarly, in the case like Azerbaijanisin Iran that live in a polyglot society, the above condition could hold true. It seems that this language is considered as the low variety and is excluded from the powerful public sphere and relegated to informal and family domains, whereas Persian dominates education and literature. Azerbaijanis in Iran have been dependent on the domination of Persian in education. "A current case of dependence is that of minority literatures. These are produced by minority groups, or by groups which are geographically connected to or politically subjugated by some (politically, economically) more powerful group "(Even-Zohar, 1990, p.56). Also, Even-Zohar (1990) stated that in the case of direct interference agents of the target literature "know the language of the source literature and may have better access to its resources than in the case of the second type [indirect interference]" (p57). Therefore, the domination of Persian seems to generate a direct interference in Azerbaijani literature in Iran.

Jaffe (2010) has emphasized the importance of translation and stated that "there is an underlying political dimension to all translations, for each act of translation posits a relationship of power between languages and cultures" (p.267). Moreover, she has focused on the function of translating a document and has claimed that:

Given the fact that not all educated Azerbaijanis of Iran speak or read Azerbaijani but all educated Azerbaijanis of Iran speak and read Persian, translating scientific text into Azerbaijani while it is available within the repertoire of official language actually will probably be regarded as an open violation. In addition, the conflict between the Azerbaijani social activists and government over the establishment of Azerbaijani schools could possibly amount to this sensitivity. Moreover, it seems that translating scientific and pedagogical books into Azerbaijani could amount to the tensions. Therefore, on the one hand, one may consider the non-existence of scientific translation and original books as a result of no need for such texts, on the other; this also could probably be treated as an open violation.

4.6. Contacts may take place with only one part of the target literature; it may then proceed to other parts.

In his 2010 version of the "Laws of Cultural Interference," Even-Zohar has stated in a footnote in page 52 that the paper is a rewriting of his previous paper "Laws of Literary Interference," *Poetics Today* 11:1, p-p 53-72 that is adapted to the field of culture. He claimed that the paper "actually transcended from the outset [of] the restricted field of 'literature' and were almost integrally applicable to the larger field of culture" (2010, p.53). Therefore, the present research developed its discussions mostly on the 1990 version of this hypothesis which directly deals with the literary interference.

In his 1990 version of "Laws of Literary Interference," Even-Zohar has claimed that "even when appropriations are 'heavy,' there is not necessarily an overall interference. Usually certain sections remain untouched, while others undergo massive invasion, or are literally created by appropriations" (p.69). He added that interference may be confined to only one stratum, and then interfere with other strata. For example a model takes place with the center of the literature and then proceeds to the periphery (1990).

To test this hypothesis in the present study two sets of data were needed. The following figures indicate the number of the imported translations by their genres over time. This set of data shows how Azerbaijani literature in Iran has imported translations from several sources since 1357. Because the dada could not be put in one figure the researcher has put them in three charts, i.e., Figures 4.8, 4.9 and 4.10.

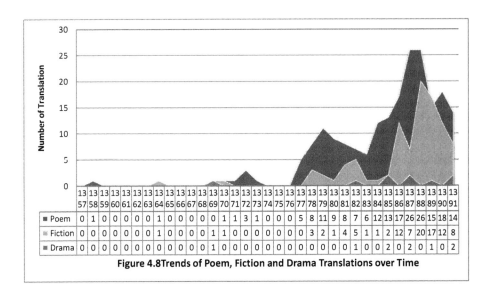

Year	1357	1358	1359	1360	1361	1362	1363	1364	1365	1366	1367	1368	1369	1370	1371	1372	1373	1374	1375	1376	1377	1378	1379	1380	1381	1382	1383	1384	1385	1386	1387	1388	1389	1390	1391
Poem	0	1	0	0	0	0	0	1	0	0	0	0	0	1	1	3	1	0	0	0	5	8	11	9	8	7	6	12	13	17	26	26	15	18	14
Fiction	0	0	0	0	0	0	0	1	0	0	0	0	1	1	0	0	0	0	0	0	0	3	2	1	4	5	1	1	2	12	7	20	17	12	8
Drama	0	0	0	0	0	0	0	0	0	0	0	0	0	1	0	0	0	0	0	0	0	0	0	0	0	0	1	0	0	2	0	2	0	1	0

Figure 4.8Trends of Poem, Fiction and Drama Translations over Time

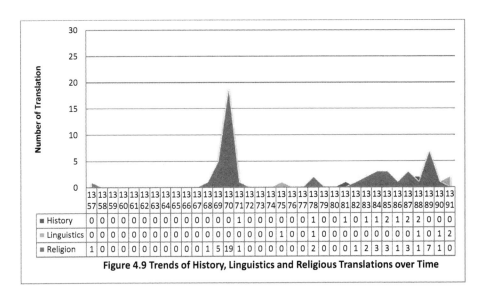

Year	1357	1358	1359	1360	1361	1362	1363	1364	1365	1366	1367	1368	1369	1370	1371	1372	1373	1374	1375	1376	1377	1378	1379	1380	1381	1382	1383	1384	1385	1386	1387	1388	1389	1390	1391
History	0	0	0	0	0	0	0	0	0	0	0	0	0	1	0	0	0	0	0	1	0	0	1	0	1	1	2	1	2	2	0	0	0		
Linguistics	0	0	0	0	0	0	0	0	0	0	0	0	0	0	0	0	0	1	0	0	1	0	0	0	0	0	0	0	1	0	1	2			
Religion	1	0	0	0	0	0	0	0	0	0	0	1	5	19	1	0	0	0	0	0	2	0	0	0	1	2	3	3	1	3	1	7	1	0	

Figure 4.9 Trends of History, Linguistics and Religious Translations over Time

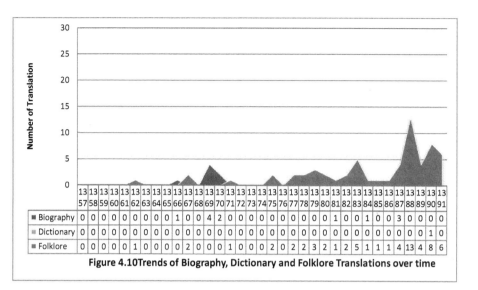

Figure 4.10 Trends of Biography, Dictionary and Folklore Translations over time

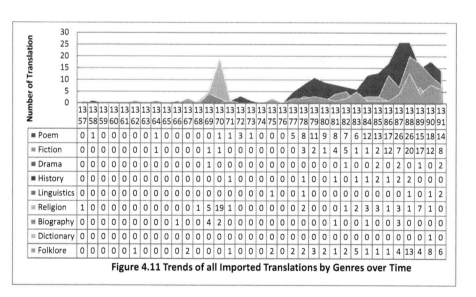

Figure 4.11 Trends of all Imported Translations by Genres over Time

75

The above figures, 4.8, 4.9, 4.10, and 4.11 indicate that translation into the literature of Azerbaijani in Iran has had a gradually increasing trend over time. It is evident that the contacts have taken place with some genres then have proceeded to other parts. For example, religion, poem and folklore translations have been the first contacts with Azerbaijani literature in Iran after the Islamic Revolution. Gradually these contacts have proceeded to other parts, like fiction and drama.

According to Nam Fung Chang (2011), one cannot judge a literary system within the framework of polysystem theory only by having a synchronic perspective. Therefore, if a researcher studies a literary system within the framework of polysystem theory, s/he needs to analyze it diachronically as well as synchronically. The delimitation of the present study did not allow the researchers to study the literary system of Azerbaijani of Iran diachronically, although the authors have attempted to comment on the basis of diachronic point of view.

Even-Zohar (2010) believed that contacts can be defined as "a relation (ship) between cultures," whereas "interference is thus a procedure emerging in the environment of contacts, one where transfer has taken place" (p.52). Consequently, he has stated that "hence, 'interference' and 'contacts' are distinct processes, definitely interconnected but not fully overlapping" (p.53). Thus, the possible contacts between two cultures can lead to interference. However, he (2010) believed that not every contact necessarily leads to interference. As a result, the research tends to find out about the possible contacts then go through the possible interferences.

According to the foregoing discussions, it seems that Azerbaijani literature in Iran is indirectly interfered with mostly by the literature of the Republic of Azerbaijan and directly by the Persian Literature, the paper has considered these two literatures as its subject of discussions. The following figure shows how translations from the literature of the Republic of Azerbaijan have taken place in the category of poem and then have proceeded to other parts.

76

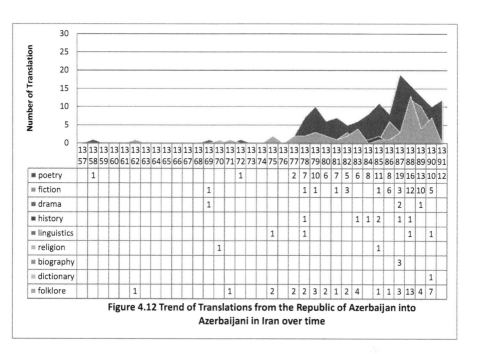

	1357	1358	1359	1360	1361	1362	1363	1364	1365	1366	1367	1368	1369	1370	1371	1372	1373	1374	1375	1376	1377	1378	1379	1380	1381	1382	1383	1384	1385	1386	1387	1388	1389	1390	1391
poetry	1													1							2	7	10	6	7	5	6	8	11	8	19	16	13	10	12
fiction													1								1	1		1	3			1	6	3	12	10	5		
drama													1																	2		1			
history																							1				1	1	2		1	1			
linguistics																			1				1									1	1		
religion													1														1								
biography																														3					
dictionary																																			1
folklore						1								1							2	2	2	3	2	1	2	4		1	1	3	13	4	7

Figure 4.12 Trend of Translations from the Republic of Azerbaijan into Azerbaijani in Iran over time

Figure 4.12 shows that the first contact has taken place in the category of poem in 1358 and then contacts have been proceeded to other genres, like folklore, fiction and drama, etc. Even-Zohar (1990) believed that "Contacts may take place with only one part of the target literature; it may then proceed to other parts" (p.69). According to the above discussion it is evident that contacts between the literature of the Republic of Azerbaijan and Azerbaijani literature in Iran have taken place with only one genre and then proceeded to other genres. In the course of time, these contacts seem to have been increased and have resulted into an indirect interference from the literature of the Republic of Azerbaijan. As discussed in the section 4.4, the contacts between the literary system of Azerbaijani in Iran and the Republic of Azerbaijan have resulted into a new form of translation, which is called "Kochurme."

77

Chapter Five:

Conclusion

5.1. Overview

In the present chapter, conclusions and implications of the research are presented. A summary of what has been done so far is provided in section 5.2. In section 5.3, the implications of the research are discussed. The concluding remarks are presented in section 5.4. Finally in section 5.5, some suggestions for further research are made.

5.2. Summary

In chapter one, the problem of the research was introduced. Studying the Azerbaijani literature in Iran as a social configuration within the laws of literary interference was defined as the problem of the study. Four questions have been introduced in the case of the literature of Azerbaijani in Iran; (a) is interference mostly unilateral? (b) Does contact eventually generate interference in the absence of resisting condition? (c) Does interference occur for the unavailable items within the literary system? (d) Does contact occur with only one part of the target literature? Even-Zohar's (2010) four hypotheses of the literary interference were selected as the framework. The purpose of the study was to examine these four hypotheses to determine whether they hold true in the case of Azerbaijani literary system in Iran. The significant, limitations and delimitations of the research have been introduced in chapter one.

Chapter two of the present research has been divided into three main sections. In the first section, an introduction of the polysystem theory as well as the laws of literary interference was provided. The second section mostly dealt with four works done within the framework of polysystem theory. Finally in the third section, background of literary and historical condition of Azerbaijani has been provided.

In chapter three, the methodology of the research was presented. The type of the research as well as the design has been explained. Moreover, the process of data collection and procedure of data analysis were stated. In chapter four, the results and findings of the data analysis were presented. Even-Zohar's (2010) laws of literary interference were selected as the framework to study the data. Finally in chapter five, the results and findings were discussed with respect to the questions of the research.

5.3. Conclusions

In the present study, four questions were posed;

a) Is interference mostly unilateral?

b) Does contact eventually generate interference in the absence of resisting condition?

c) Does interference occur for the unavailable items within the literary system?

d) Does contact occur with only one part of the target literature?

1. In the first question, the research was mainly concerned with the number of the translations into and from Azerbaijani of Iran. Azerbaijani of Iran has translated books rather from the Republic of Azerbaijan and Persian than other source languages. It was evident enough that the interference between the Azerbaijani literature in Iran and the literature of the Republic of Azerbaijan was mostly unilateral. Provided data indicated that there was a major literary interference from the literature of the Republic of Azerbaijan, whereas the literary interference from Azerbaijani in Iran was minor. The findings of the research showed that in the case of Azerbaijani of Iran interference was mostly unilateral.

2. In the second question, absence or presence of resisting conditions were the subjects of study. "Kochurme" "کوچورمه" was introduced as a resisting condition against

80

translations from Persian literature and a tendency towards the literature of the Republic of Azerbaijan. Therefore, the second hypothesis of literary interference, "Contacts will sooner or later generate interference if no resisting conditions arise," holds true in the case of the literary system of Azerbaijani in Iran.

3. In the third question, two sets of data were required. Firstly, it was needed to determine what items were available within the repertoire of Azerbaijani in Iran to judge what items were required to be imported. Secondly, the imported translations needed to be categorized by their genres to decide whether the unavailability of an item in the repertoire has been provided through translation.

Having analyzed the number of the available and unavailable items within the repertoire of Azerbaijani in Iran, the result was that this language has imported the items that were available within it.

Even-Zohar's "Interference occurs when a system is in need of items unavailable within its own repertoire" seems not to hold true in the case of Azerbaijani literary system in Iran. On the one hand, one may consider the non-existence of scientific translation and original books as a result of no need for such texts, on the other; this also could be treated as an open violation.

4. In the fourth question, the researchers studied Itamar Even-Zohar's hypothesis, which states that interference may be confined to only one stratum, and then interfere with other strata. For example a model takes place with the center of the literature and then proceeds to the periphery (1990). To test this hypothesis in the present study two sets of data were required. First, the trend of the translations by their genres over time was needed. Analyzing these data indicated that the contacts have taken place with some genres then have proceeded to other genres. For example, religious, poem and folklore translations have been the first contacts with Azerbaijani literature of Iran after the Islamic Revolution. In the course of time, these contacts have proceeded to other genres, like fiction and drama.

81

Second, the trend of the translations from the literature of the Republic of Azerbaijan by their genres over time was provided. This also showed that contacts between the literature of the Republic of Azerbaijan and Azerbaijani literature in Iran have taken place with only one genre and then proceeded to other genres .In the course of time, these contacts have been increased and have resulted into an indirect interference from the literature of the Republic of Azerbaijan, i.e., *Kochurme*.

Even-Zohaı has hypothesized that "Contacts may take place with only one part of the target literature; it may then proceed to other parts." It seems that this hypothesis holds true in the case of Azerbaijani literature in Iran.

5.4 Implications

The findings of this research would help specifically those who study the impact of translation on the literature of Azerbaijani in Iran. It also would help those who study minority languages in relation to majority languages within the framework of the polysystem theory. Moreover, the study is hoped to help the prospective students who are interested in the polysystem theory, especially the laws of literary interference. It is also hoped that the findings of the present study would delineate the outline of the Azerbaijani literary system in Iran since the Islamic Revolution.

5.5. Suggestions for Further Research

1. The present research has focused on four out of nine hypotheses of literary interference in the case of Azerbaijani literary system in Iran within the framework of polysystem theory. Researches on the rest of the hypotheses would be illuminating.

2. Other minority languages in Iran can be also studied within the methodological and conceptual framework used in this research.

3. It was found that Azerbaijani literature in Iran was indirectly interfered with by the literature of the Republic of Azerbaijan. This interference was embodied in the form of a unique type of translation called as "کوچورمه," "Kochurme." Further linguistic, cultural and translational studies on this form of translation would be illuminating.

4. The aim of the research was to study the literary system of Azerbaijani in Iran with the viewpoint of indirect interference. Also, it was discussed that Azerbaijani in Iran is often directly interfered with by Persian. Therefore, studying this case within the framework of direct interference in relation to Persian would be illuminating as well.

References

Aldridge, E.M., 2001, **Connotations in public and political discourse**, In Desblanche, L., (ed.),**Aspects of Specialised Translation,** pp. 79-87,*Paris: Maison du dictionnaire.*

Alipour, E., 2012, **Socio-Cultural Aspects of Translation into Azerbaijani in Iran: a Case of a Minority Language,** (Unpublished MA thesis).Allameh Tabataba'i University, Tehran, Iran

Atabaki, T., 2000, **Azerbaijan: Ethnicity and autonomy in twentieth-century Iran,** (2nd ed.), *London & New York: I.B. Tauris.*

Azerbaijani people, (n.d.), Retrieved October 3, 2012 from the Wikipedia: http://en.wikipedia.org/wiki/azerbaijnai_people

Bassnett, S., 1998, **The Translation Turn in Cultural Studies,** Bassnett, s., & Lefevere, L.,**Constructing Cultures: Essays on Literary Translation,***Clevedon: Multilingual Matters.*123-140.

Birjandi, P., & Mosallanejad, P., 2005, **Research methods & principles 1 & 2,** *Tehran: Moasseseye Kheiriyeye Amuzeshi farhangi Shahid Mahdavi.*

Bosworth, C.E., 1987, December 15, **Azerbaijan iv. Islamic history to 1941,** In **Encyclopedia Iranica online,**retrieved from: http://www.iranica.com/articles /Azerbaijani-iv

Buranç A, & Alkaya, E., (2009). **Çagdaş Türk Lehçeleri.** Ankara: Akçağ.

Nam FungCh., 2001, **Polysystem Theory: Its Prospect As a Framework for Translation Research,**Target 13: 2, 317-332.

Cornell, S. E., 2011, **Azerbaijan since independence,***New York: M.E. Sharpe.*

Cronin, M., 2009, **Minority,** In Baker, M., &Saldanha, G., (eds.), **Routledgeencyclopedia of translation studies,** pp. 169-171, *Abingdon & New York: Routledge*

Dongfeng, W., 2008, **When a Turning Occurs: Counter-evidence to Polysytem Hypothesis,** In Ning,W., & Yifeng, S., (Eds), **Topics in Translation,** (35),140-154.

Edwards, J., 2010, **Minority languages and group identity: cases and categories,***Amsterdam & Philadelphia: John Benjamins B. V.*

Eker, S., 2010, **Çağdaş Türk Dili,***Ankara: Grafiker.*

Even-Zohar, I., 1978, **Papers in Historical Poetics,***Tel Aviv, The Porter Institute for Poetics and Semiotics.*

Even-Zohar, I., 1990, **Introduction [to Polysystem Theory],** *Polysystem Studies* [=Poetics Today 11:1 (1990), pp. 1-6.

Even-Zohar, I., 1990, **Laws of Literary Interference,** *Polysystem Studies* [=Poetics Today 11:1 (1990)], pp. 53-72.

Even-Zohar, I., 2010, **Papers in Culture Research,***Tel Aviv : Unit of Culture Research, Tel Aviv University.*

Even-Zohar, I., 1990, **Polysystem Theory,** in *Polysystem Studies,* [= Poetics Today 11:1], 1990, pp. 9-26.

Even-Zohar, I., 1990, **The 'Literary System',** in *Polysystem Studies* [=Poetics Today 11:1 (1990), pp. 27-44.

Even-Zohar, I., 1990, **Translation and Transfer,***Polysystem Studies* [=Poetics Today 11:1 (1990), pp. 73-78.

Even-Zohar, I., 1997a., **Polysystem Theory,***Revised version.* in idem. *Papers in Culture Research* 2004. Retrieved from: http://www.tau.ac.il/~itamarez/works/books/ez-cr2004.pdf

Even-Zohar, I., 1990a. **"The Position of Translated Literature within the Literary Polysystem".** *Polysystem Studies, Poetics Today* 11:1. 45-51. Also in Lawrence Venuti (ed.). *The Translation Studies Reader.* London and New York: Routledge, 2000. 192-197.

Even-Zohar, I. 1990c. **"System, Dynamics, and Interference in Culture: A Synoptic View".** *Polysystem Studies, Poetics Today* 11:1. 85-95.

Even-Zohar, I., 1990c. **"Translation and Transfer."** In; idem, *Polysystem Studies (=Poetics Today* 11:1, 73-78.

Even-Zohar, I., 2002. "**Culture Planning and Cultural Resistance in the Making and Maintaining of Entities**." *Sun Yat-Sen Journal of Humanities* 14. 45-52. Also in Itamar Even-Zohar. 2004. *Papers in Culture Research*. Web: http://www.tau.ac.il/~itamarez. 104-113.

Even-Zohar, I., 2004. "**Culture Planning**" (revised version of Itamar Even-Zohar 1996. "Culture Planning and the Market: Making and Maintaining Socio-semiotic Entities"). *Papers in Culture Research*. Web: http://www.tau.ac.il/~itamarez. 82-103.

Farhady, H., (2009). **Research methods in applied linguistics 1 & 2**. Iran: Payam Nour University.

González, M. G., (2005). **Translation of minority languages in bilingual and multilingual communities**. In A. Branchadell., L. M. West (Eds.), Less translated languages (pp. 105-123). Amsterdam/Philadelphia: John Benjamins Publishing Company.

Hermans, T., 1999. *Translation in Systems: Descriptive and System-oriented Approaches Explained*. Manchester: St. Jerome.

Hogan-Brun, G., & Wolff, S. (2003). **Minority languages in Europe: an introduction to the current debate**. In G. Hogan-Brun & Wolf (eds.), Minority languages in Europe: frameworks, status, prospects (pp. 3-15). Hampshire and New York: Palgrave Macmillan.

Jaffe, A., (2010). **Locating power: Corsican translators and their critics.** In M. Baker (Ed.), Critical readings in translation studies (pp. 263-282). London and New York: Routledge.

Kayyal, M., (2008). **Interference of the Hebrew language in translations from modern Hebrew literature into Arabic.** *Benjamins Translation Library, (75), 33-50.*

Lefevere, A., 1992. *Translation, Rewriting, & the Manipulation of Literary Fame.* London and New York: Routledge.

Maghsoudi, M., (2001). **Tahavolat-e gomi dar Iran: elal va zamineha** [Ethnic evolutions in Iran: causes and grounds]. Tehran: Moassese-ye Motale'ate Melli.

Matsunaga-Watson, N., (2005). **The Selection of texts for translation in postwar Japan: An Examination of One Aspect of Polysystem Theory.** In E. Hung (Ed), *Benjamins Translation Library, (61), 161-173.*

Munday, J. (2002) Systems in translation: **A systemic model for descriptive translation studies.** In T. Hermans (ed.) (2002) *Crosscultural Transgressions: ResearchModels in Translation Studies II: Historical and Ideological Issues* (pp. 76-92). Manchester: St Jerome Press.

Novin, H. (2011/1390). **Tarikh-e azeri dar Azerbaijan** [The history of Azeri language in Azerbaijan]. Tehran: Entesharat-e Tamadon-e Irani.

Presidential Library. **Administrative Department of the President of the Republic of Azerbaijan.** Retrieved January 20, 2013, from http://files.preslib.az/projects/remz/pdf_en/atr_dil.pdf

User,Ş. H., (2006). **Başlangıcından Günümüze Türk Yazı Sistemleri, Sosyo-Kültürel Bir Yaklaşım.** Ankara: Akçağ.

Rashedi, H. (2007/1386). **Torkan va barresi-ye arikh, zaban va hoviyat-e anha dar Iran** [=Turks and an analysis of their history, language and identity in Iran]. Tehran: Andisheye No.

Shaffer, B. (2000). **The formation of Azerbaijani collective identity in Iran.** Nationalities Papers, 28(3), 449-477.

Shaffer, B. (2002). **Borders and brethren: Iran and the challenge of Azerbaijani identity.** Cambridge: MIT press.

Shuttleworth, M. (2011). **Polysystem.** In M.Baker & G. Saldanha (eds.), Routledge encyclopedia of translation studies (pp. 197-200). London & New York: Routledge.

Snell-Hornby, M. Pochhacker, F. and Kaindl, K. (eds) (1994) *Translation Studies: An Interdiscipline.* Amsterdam: John Benjamins.

Toury, G. (1978) **The nature and role of norms in literary translation.** In J. Holmes, J.Lambert, R. Van den Broeck (eds) *Literature and Translation: New Perspectives inLiterary Studies.* Leuven: ACCO.

Toury, G. 1995. *Descriptive Translation Studies and Beyond*. Amsterdam/Philadelphia: John Benjamins.

Venuti, L. (1998a) Introduction. In L. Venuti (ed.) *Translation and Minority*. Special issue of *The Translator* 4 (2), 135-144.

Verdoodt, A., Kloss, H. & McConnel, G. D. (1989). **Europe occidentale: les langues regionals et minoritaires des pays membres du Conseil de l'Europe**. Québec: Les Presses del'Université Laval.

Williams, J., & Chesterman, A. (2002). **The Map: a beginner's guide to doing research in translation studies**. Great Britain: St. Jerome Publishing.

Printed in Great Britain
by Amazon

82364851R00059